There Is More!

There Is More!

8 STEPS TO EMBRACING THE GREATER YOU

Niki Brown

ISBN 0692510443
ISBN 13: 9780692510445
Printed in the United States of America
Publisher: Purpose by Design, LLC
First Edition: October 2015
Editor: Bob Hostetler
Cover Photography: Ed Ward Photography
Cover design: Bev Cotton/Bev Cotton Designs
Some names and identifying details of clients have been changed to protect their identities.

Dedication

This book is dedicated to Sara McCullough and all the Sara's she left behind. You were a mentor, spiritual mom and friend, not just to me but to countless others. You are the embodiment of grace, beauty, courage and the idea that it's never too late to begin again. While you achieved much, and impacted many, I still believe you were gone too soon.

Praise for *There Is More!*

———— ◌◌◌ ————

Niki Brown's passion and wisdom are contagious. Everyone should catch what she has, and once you start reading *There Is More*, you'll be infected with her positive, empowering message.

—Bob Hostetler, Bestselling author of *The Red Letter Life*.
www.bobhostetler.com

"Within these pages, Niki Brown lays out a plan for becoming the best version of yourself. She clearly articulates how to hit the bulls' eye that was ordained just for you. After 30 years in human services, finding ways to empower people to take back their lives and make a difference has become a primary mission. Niki Brown shares a no holds barred pathway to finding mission and "fulfilling it."

—Chris Groeber, MSW, CEO; Key Assets Kentucky

A modern-day approach to The Purpose Driven Life, Reverend Niki Brown fascinates with a step by step guide to unlocking our seen and unseen purpose and passions. *There Is More* delivers with transparent and compassionate life examples that will thrust one into realizing the greatness that resides in each of us.

—Minister Kim Young Woods, M.Ed.,
Founder of LifeChangers Ministries

"From sharing her own powerful story of being trapped in a dream to showing you how to activate your God intended purpose, Niki Brown's new book, *There Is More*, will leave you inspired and equipped to receive the "more" that is destined for your life. So many people talk about wanting more, but very few know how to achieve it. Niki has crafted a life guide which points women in the direction of the life they crave. This book is filled with energy and passion! You'll find a fresh revelation and reminder in its pages that the life you have been waiting on…is actually waiting on you. It's your season. It's your time. Go get your blessing! This book will help you get there.

—Dr. Jevonnah "Lady J" Ellison, Founder
of Maximum Potential Academy;
Author of ***You Have What It Takes***
www.jevonnah.com

"After reading "*There is More! 8 Steps To Embracing The Greater You*," I am so inspired and determined to channel my energy to make my life all it was meant to be. This book has challenged me to be all that God has designed for me to be. Everyone should not only read this book, but use it as a tool to make their lives extraordinary. I have met the author and after hearing her speak, I am in awe of her knowledge and outlook. She is an amazing, inspiring and engaging lady!"

—Sandy C. Romenesko, Executive Director,
Mt. Sterling-Montgomery County
Industrial Authority and Chamber of Commerce

"There really is more for your life than what you imagined. Niki Brown's magnificent work challenges you to realize the life you desire happens intentionally not automatically. Her eight step coaching strategy will move your life from basic to brilliant."

—Dr. Johnny Parker, Former Chaplain of Washington Redskins
Author of Renovating Your Marriage
www.johnnyparker.com

From the onset, Niki Brown looked into my soul and exposed my dreams and fears. The book is divided into two sections in which Niki uses the acronym PATH to identify four steps to realizing "the greater you" along with owning and embracing individual greatness. Using her distinctive coaching style guided by her strong faith, Niki motivates and empowers women to find their passion and make it a reality.

—Carol Siler, Executive Director,
Women Leading Kentucky

Many people live an unfulfilled life due to fears, limiting beliefs, doubts, past hurts and living up to other people's expectations. Niki Brown has revealed the steps to living a fulfilled life by taking you on an 8 step journey that will help you get on a P.A.T.H that will quench the silent thirst for "more." This book will encourage you to dust off your vision, step out on faith, walk into your greatness and live your God intended life.

—Sheila Belle, Coach, Speaker and Entrepreneur
www.sheilabelle.com

Powerful! Insightful! Put this on the shelf next to the greats in the Self-Improvement genre. There Is More reaches into the heart, mind and soul of the reader and challenges you to go beyond the status quo. Niki Brown designs a life-transforming message and game plan that will resonate with any reader seeking truth and affirmation that your life has value and worth.

—Renai Ellison, Founder and CEO
Renai Ellison Coaching & Training, LLC.
www.renaiellison.com

This book provides immense insight. It is NOT a self- help book, this is a transformational action guide. Please get ready to work on you. She challenges us to live higher, live on purpose, and to extend our reach and help others. You will be inspired....You will be Challenged, You will be MOVED... To be a Greater YOU!

—Felicia Houston, MA, LCPC, CWA,
Founder, Anointed Wives Ministry (AWM)
http://www.anointedwivesministry.com

In *There Is More*, Niki Brown not only shows you how to discover your purpose, but she also takes you where many won't by telling you how to put action to your words and thoughts! If you are a woman who desires more, this book serves as a blueprint for next level living.

—Lamar Tyler, Tyler New Media; 2012
Ebony Power 100 Honoree
BlackandMarriedWithKids.com
ltyler@tylernewmedia.com

Acknowledgements

———— ❧ ————

L IKE MOST AUTHORS WHO EMBARK on writing and publishing their first book–it was a huge undertaking where the process seemed to outweigh the future benefits. But there were so many people who kept me encouraged, inspired and anchored along the way. I am positive that I would not have completed this assignment without their presence in my life.

First, I thank God for enticing me to move beyond my own boundaries, limitations and fears. Your constant presence through all of my faults is a daily reminder that your love and favor are enough.

To my husband, best friend, lover and my champion-Harold. Your love, support, consistency and calm is everything to me. I love you. Myka thank you for sharing your dreams for how successful you thought my book will be! You inspire me. Mommy loves you!

Thanks to my family, brothers, and parents Ronald and Pat Walker–for your endless love and support and most importantly for teaching me how to walk with God. Ronald thank you for being my sounding board and always understanding my heart.

I could not function without my "besties" and "ride or die" crew: Melody, Myka, Lisa, Anita, Sandy, Tamera J., Ronda and Courtney. I am the sister, counselor, friend, mother and wife because of you. Myka W. thank you for allowing me to practice the PATH on you and being my constant cheerleader throughout this entire process.

Thanks to Lisa Evans, Yalonda Gambrell, Kelly Mobley, June White and the entire women's department at Bethany Baptist Church. My women's ministry was born because of you.

My Purpose by Design team rocks! Thanks for following me into the unknown and believing in the "more" before I did.

Thanks to my editor, Bob Hostetler. Your ability to put your finger on the pulse of my thoughts is amazing. You are an amazing author and editor. Thank you for teaching me to not just write words, but to tell a story.

Dr. Harold Arnold and my mastermind group, *The Influentials*, you have truly inspired me to reach beyond my comfort zone this year.

To my new Lexington, Kentucky church family, Total Grace. Pastor Mike and Lady Erin Robinson, you are both phenomenal trailblazers. Thank you for embracing my family as if you have known us forever. We are honored to serve in your ministry.

Chris & Jeannette Groeber, you will never know how your presence in our lives confirmed God's purpose for us being here in Kentucky. Kim & Torrey Woods, Sandy Romenesko, Janet Kenney and Carol Siler, thank you for unselfishly sharing what you have with me.

Finally, I want to thank Bishop David Evans of Bethany Baptist Church. You took me under your wing over 20 years ago because you believed in my gift, when I didn't have the faith to believe in it for myself. But through your teaching, mentoring and tough love (smile), a "greater me" was born.

Table of Contents

Section Two: Embrace "The Greater You"

Introduction
There Is More!

———— ✒︎ ————

FOUR WORDS CAN CHANGE YOUR life forever, if you allow them: *I just want more.*

These were my exact thoughts the day I finally acknowledged the truth: the person I had become was an illusion. It was an inner knowing I secretly carried for years, but was too afraid to acknowledge. In spite of my educational achievements and many accomplishments, my life was a mere shell of what I truly desired. It was a life that had been built around the opinion and perception of everyone but me, a life in which my past pain and mistakes limited my thinking, handicapped my vision, and disabled my ability to tap into a greater me.

Have you ever come to that kind of crossroad, one at which you realize that your external life is—and possibly always has been—out of sync with the internal rhythm and heartbeat of who you should be? A place where there is a palpable sense of something greater in existence, yet you struggle to bring it to fruition?

You may be like a runner who consistently crosses the finish line in first place, but amid the cheers and accolades you silently wonder, *what am I still missing?* How often have you felt the emptiness that comes with victory and achievement? You have conquered the mountain yet spiritually you are still seeking more.

What are you *still* missing? The answer could be everything… and nothing! Sometimes we miss seeing that the very things that were designed to make our lives fulfilling are also things that feel burdensome and painful. Or you could be missing the opportunity to live out your real passion because you have been told that it just isn't "practical." What you may be missing is the truth that no matter how much you have achieved or how much you have yet to achieve; you were born for more.

On the other hand, however, you are missing absolutely nothing. Because locked within your DNA is a gift, talent, ability, idea, and resource that was intended to make your life great. In other words, you were born fully loaded. Nothing missing, nothing lacking. Your background, past experiences, and the neighborhood and family in which you were raised cannot change the structure or substance of your inherent potential. This is what I call "the greater you." It's the part of you that is resilient and has survived despite obstacles, setbacks, mistakes, detours and even success. It's the principle at work in your life that has the ability to exceed and overcome every human limitation if you allow it. Sadly, however, "the greater you" is also the part of you that has probably gone uncultivated due to fear, neglect, and misunderstanding.

The idea that we carry greatness within us can seem so abstract and subjective. What does greatness really look like? The word great is defined as being "above average; exceptional."[1] I would like to define it as "living life at your fullest and highest capacity, transcending expectation, and fully embracing every known and unknown gift, skill, talent, resource and purpose."

All of us have something exceptional connected to our lives. That something or above-average quality is called greatness.

Greatness begins as a seed. What we do with that seed is determined by how we perceive it. To the natural eye it appears minuscule and mundane. But I am convinced that God likes to hide big things in small packages. He specializes in placing uncommon goals, dreams, and talents in common people. Jesus was the Son of God, but he lived on earth as the son of a common carpenter. From all appearances he had an ordinary background and upbringing, but he carried within himself an exceptional purpose—to redeem the entire world.

To discover and embrace "the greater you" means that you must do the antithesis and accept the part of you that appears small. You must own what looks and feels insignificant and determine to do something extraordinary with it. This means you will need to embrace those heartbreaking and painful experiences in your past and deliberately look for purpose and meaning in them. You will have to go back and recover those ideas and dreams you tossed to the side because they were deemed "not good enough" by yourself or others. In doing this you will not find less; you will actually discover more.

Jesus taught this principle to his disciples in the Parable of the Talents.[2] He told a story of a property owner who gave each of his servants a sum of money in talents, the largest monetary unit of the day. To one he gave five talents, to another two, and to another one. The servants understood that they were to manage these talents wisely, in ways which would result in a return on the owner's investment in them. The man who was given five talents invested it and produced five more. The servant who was given two did the same. But the servant who was given only one talent took it and hid it in the ground. When the master came and asked why he hid his talent, the servant responded that he was afraid he wouldn't be able to measure up to the standard his master had for him. In other words, he was afraid he would fail. So instead of taking the risk of producing more, he preferred the safety of mediocrity and held onto what he had been given.

This parable reveals an important truth about achieving greatness. A life of greatness doesn't just arrive on your doorstep; you must create it. If you have the requisite courage, drive, tenacity, and faith, the abundant life is available. Many people often spiritualize mediocrity and fear by saying, "I'm just waiting on God to open a door for me," or "God knows what's best for me, I'm just waiting for Him to show me what to do."

Although God creates our destiny and points the way, He expects us to build a bridge to get there. In other words, it is our responsibility to dig beneath the surface of our ordinary lives and discover those innate talents, resources, gifts, skills, and capacities that will shift us from "good" to "exceptional."

A second truth is that a life of greatness must show up in your mind and heart before it will materialize in your hand. As I look at the parable, my sense is that the servant who received the single talent didn't see the value and potential in what he was given. He hid behind excuses and even blamed his master, in effect, for why he couldn't do more. But the truth is, he didn't believe or perceive of his ability to create greatness. He viewed his one talent as being insignificant, rather than ingredients for increase.

I am convinced that God moves most often—and most powerfully—in the realm of perspective. I have coached and counseled many women who blamed their difficult childhood or a lack of resources for their lack of success in obtaining or achieving more. And when they saw someone who seemed to have what they wanted, they would assume that person had a better upbringing or some kind of head start on them. But notice that the parable never distinguishes between the servants' backgrounds or advantages. In fact, Jesus said specifically that each one received according to what they could handle, with the expectation for them to create increase.[3]

Believe me, I understand the one-talent servant well. For years I prayed to God to give me more and allow me to *be* more when, in reality, I was asking for what I already had. My inability to see the potential in who I was and what I had been given prevented me from creating the life I desired. I hid for years behind the excuse that my talent was not good enough, and that I didn't have the resources I needed to do more. I couldn't see what I carried because just like a human embryo, the embryo of greatness is invisible to the natural eye. But the moment I perceived of my own seed potential and acknowledged it, God empowered me to do more with what I had.

Your perception of what you have, determines what you create. Unfortunately, many of us can identify with this servant. We wait for outside confirmation of an internal reality. We pursue purpose and affirmation from people and places only to discover we already have it. We work to earn favor with men, when in truth all we need is to embrace our favor with God.

How do we tap into the "more" of which we are capable? How do we create the life we desire? To many people, "more" means strictly—or largely—materialistic gain—that is, how much you have in the bank or how many cars you own (or how big or nice those cars are!). But you can have all of this...and still not have more. I have worked with people who had these things, yet cried themselves to sleep every night because of their emptiness of heart. This quest for "more" of which I speak and write is not a pursuit of mere possessions, but rather a journey inside ourselves to pull out something that can't be purchased or built with money. It's an arousal of those dormant places in our lives that we have not cultivated due to fear, doubt, insecurity, lack of time, or because we just didn't know the possibility of more existed.

Embracing "the greater you" means choosing to live at your fullest capacity and potential. It means deciding—whether you have one idea, talent, or gift…or several—to maximize what you have to increase your sense of fulfillment in life and extend your reach in order to impact others.

———&———

How This Book Works

There Is More is a life guide that teaches women how to take ownership of their God-given potential and talents in order to create a life of abundance. It is designed to help you take responsibility for the self-imposed roadblocks and limitations, as well as outside forces that hinder you from seeing and creating more. And while being financially secure is a part of achieving greatness, I agree with author Harvey Makay that "being rich is a state of mind."[4] Therefore, the principles and ideas in this book will not necessarily teach you to how to get more money, but will guide you into discovering the ingredients of increase you already carry within you—and how to put them to work. Even more, these pages will teach you that success is an "inside job,"—that to be rich you must live from the inside out—and take the internal presence of greatness and turn it into an external reality of purpose, joy, power, esteem, and security in your life.

There Is More is separated into two sections. The first section of the book will teach you the four steps to discovering "the greater you." Together these steps form the acronym, PATH: Pursue purpose and passion, Authenticate your life, Transform your perspective, and Harness your potential.

SECTION ONE

STEP 1: PURSUE PURPOSE AND PASSION

This section lays the foundation for discovering "the greater you" and begins with purpose. Your life rises and falls on the ability to recognize and live out your mission and deepest passions. Chapters one and two develop the idea that purpose and passion are the "central command stations" of your life, the heartbeat for the instinctual drive to do what you love most. But purpose is not just the discovery of your assignments; it's the discovery of *you*. It's the discovery of "the greater you."

STEP 2: AUTHENTICATE YOUR LIFE

This section is designed to help you embrace your authentic self by examining those forces that hinder you from living out the truth. Your truth. You will learn that authenticity takes courage. It requires you to be willing to step out of the shadows and onto the stage of your true identity. For those bold enough to be themselves; they will discover the victory that comes with authentic living.

STEP 3: TRANSFORM YOUR PAST PERSPECTIVE

Chapters four through five begin by challenging you to change your perspective regarding your past experiences. A negative past can often make you question your ability to step into a greater future. Discovering "the greater you" requires you to become a student of your past. In doing so, you will learn that every experience had a purpose in shaping you into the woman you are now. You will also find that the seeds of greatness you carry within you, were actually developed *because* of your past, not in spite of it. The last half of this step will take you through the recovery process and equip you to build vulnerable, transparent, and authentic relationships even at the risk of being hurt again.

STEP 4: HARNESS YOUR POTENTIAL

This section closes the first half of the book by laying out three critical laws that will help you to harness your potential. These three laws reveal how relationships, environment, and process can either hinder your potential or help you build launching pads into your future. These laws were developed from my own personal experiences as well as the experiences of those I have counseled. These chapters—six through eight—are designed to challenge your vision to find potential in where you are and how it can influence developing "the greater you."

SECTION TWO

The second half of the book will help you own and embrace "the greater you" by taking you through the last four steps of the **PATH**: Prioritize your assignments, Activate your God intentions, Trust the transition, and Harvest the moment.

STEP 5: PRIORITIZE YOUR ASSIGNMENTS

Chapter nine will empower the woman who wants to live a life of intentional greatness. You will learn key steps in how to prioritize your time and assignments. You will learn time-honored principles for saying "no" to things that drain you of your life energy and deplete your passion to create more. You will be empowered to learn new techniques in clarifying your focus and adjusting your priorities to enable you to fulfill your life's passion and purpose. You'll no longer be willing to allow others to define your priorities and agenda, but will more highly value and more wisely use your time in pursuit of "the greater you."

STEP 6: ACTIVATE YOUR GOD INTENTIONS

Chapters ten through twelve will help you take deliberate action in creating the life you desire and want. These pages will motivate you to take the steps necessary to overcome fear, procrastination, and aimlessness. They will help you get out of your own way so that your "God intentions"—much more powerful than mere *good* intentions—can be activated. Your God intentions are those dreams, plans, or goals that you feel a God-given stirring to do, but still haven't gotten to. You will acquire tools for aligning your intentions and faith to produce action.

STEP 7: TRUST THE TRANSITION

This section is designed to help you manage seasons of transition. Transitions are never easy as we have to move away from what was comfortable and familiar and move toward uncertainty. In the uncertainty however, there is a certainty that a "greater you" is emerging. If we allow it, transition can shift us into new levels of faith, opportunity, and dependence on God.

STEP 8: HARVEST YOUR MOMENT

These chapters—fifteen and sixteen—will motivate you to look with the eyes of faith into your future, and plan in advance for what is coming. We can't always predict exactly which doors and opportunities will be presented to us, but we can plan for them nonetheless. Being intentional about living a life of greatness means living in "ready mode." We can't stumble into greatness; we have to schedule ourselves into it. In these chapters, I will teach you about "SMART" goals which help you to develop a plan of action, and build a timeline for achieving them.

Along the way, each chapter in *There Is More* will incorporate:

* Biblical or spiritual principles.
* An inspirational profile of someone who symbolizes the step.
* Practical strategies to achieving the step.
* A skill-builders section after each chapter with reflection questions to help stimulate critical thinking and change.

Finally, a personal note. I wrote *There Is More,* to inspire you to believe in "now." It is written with the intention to help you time-shift from just dreaming about having more in your future, to manifesting more in your present. For years, I have watched women—including myself—wait for *others* to grant us permission to truly live and pursue our hearts' passions, when we should be purposefully designing our lives in partnership with the God who made us—and implanted greatness within us.

A good friend of mine embodied this truth. Sara and I attended graduate school together. She was in her late sixties when we became friends, and I admired her drive and determination to stay up with all of us "young people," as she called us. After she obtained her master's degree, she immediately went on to pursue her doctorate. When she finished her dissertation, we all celebrated her accomplishment. A week after receiving her doctorate, she went into the hospital for a simple knee replacement. The surgery was a success, but my friend Sara never came home. Following the surgery, a blood clot traveled to her heart. She died instantly.

I was devastated. I questioned God. She had just started living her dreams. Why would God take her like that? Is that how my life would be? Would I work so hard to achieve, to reach my goals, only to have God cut my time short? But then one day I sensed God answering my questions. In answer to my complaints and accusations, I believe He said, "I didn't cut her time short; it was *she* who waited to live her dreams."

God gives you and I the freedom to do whatever we desire with the time allotted to us on this earth. He gives us the choice in how, when, or even *if* we choose to pursue our passions and dreams. My friend Sara waited most of her life for the "right moment" to go back to school and pursue her lifelong goals. She wanted to make sure everyone else's needs were met before she attended to her own needs. She helped to build the dreams of others, but left too little time to build her own.

Greatness is not achieved by those who wait for a special moment to arrive or for opportunity to knock on their door. You don't have to wait for your credit to get better, your bank account to be full, or your relationships to improve before you can live your dreams. Your ability to step into "the greater you" is created out of what you already have, with the time you've already been given. I hope this book will ignite you to move and take action, right now. Because the truth is, if you've been waiting on God to give you more, He's been waiting on you to make a move and *create* more. And if you choose, you can start right now.

Section One
Discover "The Greater You"

Step 1
Pursue Your Purpose
& Passion

CHAPTER 1

Your Existence is Proof

—⟡—

"Your purpose in life is to find your purpose and
give your whole heart and soul to it"

(GAUTAMA BUDDHA).

YOUR ARRIVAL ON EARTH WAS not by accident. It was a result of a carefully orchestrated plan by a power greater than yourself. You probably sense this because you've had several experiences throughout your life that seemed too coordinated to call them coincidences. No, those life experiences were divine moments.

You are probably also aware of a silent yet persistent yearning for your life to take on a deeper, more substantial, meaning. The desire is powerful, perhaps too much to put into words. Few people, know how to act on these yearnings, even if they are aware of them.

For countless years, society seems to have undertaken an intense quest to discover the true reason for our existence on earth. Authors have written hundreds of books, journals, workbooks, and seminars to help people answer this question and satisfy the thirst for meaning that exists within all of us.

A person may have a wonderful career, a comfortable home, rewarding hobbies, and a loving family, and still wonder if his or her life counts for anything. Whatever achievements they may have experienced, they may still wonder, "Does my life amount to anything? Am I doing what I was put on this earth to do? Will I leave behind anything to let the world know I was here?"

———— ∞∞ ————

Why do we have such an intense need to discover the reason for our existence? Twentieth-century philosopher Paul Tillich states, "In order to be spiritually creative…one must be able to participate meaningfully in their original creations."[5] In other words we want to belong. We want to matter. We are afraid of living a life of insignificance and invisibility. We crave purpose. Each of us wants to know that in spite of all the mishaps, painful events, and poor decisions we've made, our lives are greater than the sum of our experiences. We long to believe that our lives are destined for more.

Discovering "the greater you" begins with purpose. But discovering purpose can be a daunting task. Where do you even begin? How do you proceed? Which direction should you go? And even if you have a sense of your unique gifts, skills, and talents, how do you distinguish which of those point to your purpose?

For those who've had a difficult childhood, the task can seem even more hopeless. When you've had a painful history, the idea that you've been put on earth to do something important or impactful can seem laughable, perhaps, or too painful to embrace.

But the need to discover one's purpose runs deep and is persistent. Without purpose, your life feels superficial, hollow, and empty. Without a sense of purpose, you will go through the motions of life without really *experiencing* life. You will become trapped within the limitations of your environment, always sensing there is more, yet being unable to define or reach it.

And, more likely than not, if you don't understand and pursue your purpose, somebody will give you one to follow, that will lead you further away from your true purpose and "the greater you."

PURPOSE IN PLAIN SIGHT

But, what if your purpose doesn't need to be "discovered" because it was never hidden? What if you didn't have to "discover" it because you've already been fulfilling it? Before we move forward and explore this thought further, I would like to define purpose in the following way: *purpose is that innate assignment that confirms and qualifies your existence on Earth.*

Purpose is innate. It is the sole reason you have been created. I find it hard to believe that something this powerful, which qualifies your existence on earth, would be hidden and not acted upon until its discovery. I believe purpose is practiced at various points throughout your life and sometimes on a consistent basis. Most of us miss it because we have been taught that we have to discover our purpose first and then do it. There are even strategies to discovering what you like to do or are passionate about and then doing them more. But what happens to the person who is multi-gifted and talented, or the one who has a ton of business ideas and passions, or the person who simply has no clue at all? Those people will find it very challenging to determine their core mission on Earth.

The second reason I believe we miss purpose is that we operate in it with such consistency that it has become a natural component of our lives. We never identify it as purpose because it feels like second nature. Consequently, we dismiss what we naturally do because it feels normal, when it's really extraordinary. You don't need to go in search for your mission in life. If you take a moment and study yourself, you'll learn that your purpose is waiting to be recognized, not revealed.

For years I lived with the assumption that I needed to discover my life purpose. I read and studied books, talked to anyone who would listen, prayed and cried–and prayed some more. After years of intense soul-searching, I finally learned one single life-changing principle: my purpose was never hidden. It was there all the time, present, alive, and active in my life. It was somewhat alarming because I had been hoping to discover some awe-inspiring life assignment or task that was going to bring a sense of amazement and wonder. Instead of amazement, the answer generated a sense of familiarity. What God had purposed and planned for me was something I had been doing my entire life, but had never been aware of. While I was looking to discover purpose, purpose was waiting for me to discover myself. You don't discover your purpose and do it; you discern what you are doing and thus define your purpose.

When you discover purpose, you discover *you*. Better put, you discover "the greater part of you." You discover that innate, God-given quality that sets you apart from the rest of the world. You discover the reason your passion burns intensely for those things you can't explain. Most importantly, you discover the things you've already been doing, and start to do them better. I believe sometimes God wants us to understand this simple truth: life's journey is not a quest to find your ultimate purpose, as much as it is about you understanding who God has created you to be and how you can live out aspects of that divine revelation each and every day.

MISSION VS ASSIGNMENT

Many people believe that the discovery of purpose is the discovery of one singular task or assignment. On some level this is true, purpose will point you in the direction of your assignments in life. For some people, it's easier to associate their purpose within the context of one assignment or task and believe it to be their ultimate destiny in life. However if that particular task is no longer available, they often struggle to shift and adjust into a new one.

I counseled a young woman named Terry who believed that her purpose was to be an accountant. She obtained her Master's Degree and subsequently got a job working as an accountant. However when her job downsized several years later, Terry was unable to find steady employment. As a result, she became extremely depressed and despondent. She believed that her purpose in life was to be an accountant, yet because she was unable to operate in this field, she questioned herself and God.

After working with Terry for a while she eventually learned that her purpose was bigger than just finding a job as an accountant. Terry learned her true purpose was something she had been doing well before receiving any of her degrees; to empower people to be financially independent. Terry opened up her own business as a financial consultant and has redefined her life.

Living your purpose is greater than just one particular assignment. Purpose is your overall mission. Purpose is that inborn, instinctual drive and desire to follow a certain path or tendency.

To explain it further, purpose will answer the "what," and "why" in your life. What do you consistently do that is impactful? Why do you do it? What makes you operate in your gifts and talents? What result do you want to achieve each time? Purpose is your motivation for doing what you do.

PIECING TOGETHER PURPOSE

Several clear indicators will help you identify the purpose you've already been fulfilling.

First, purpose is connected to your predominant gift or talent. Most of us have several gifts and talents. Some you may be aware of and others are still lying dormant. For most of us, however, there is one gift that dominates. I call this your *center*. Your center is the central command station of your life. It represents the core of who you are and what you do, naturally and instinctively. It is a signature gift that you do well— almost near perfection—each time you do it. You may have been operating in this gift so often that it doesn't seem like a gift or talent to you. It seems normal and on some level you think everyone can probably do what you do; it surprises you when you learn they can't. This gift is unique to you. It is directly attached to your mission in life.

Many books and website assessments offer help for discerning your gifts. I suggest, *Now Discover Your Strengths* by Marcus Buckingham. It is an insightful read and offers a thorough assessment of your gifts and abilities.

One gift will stands out from the rest. Discover that predominant gift and it will lead you to identifying your purpose. I typically have my clients draw a diagram resembling a bicycle wheel. In the middle of the wheel is a circle (see diagram 1).

Arrows like spokes point out from the center to the outer rim. In the center of that circle you place your predominant gift, the gift you have been operating in most of your life. To get a blank copy of this wheel visit my website: www.nikibrown.org/thereismore.

FIGURE 1

For example, my center on the diagram is empowerment. I used to believe that teaching was my center, but teaching is a learned skill; it takes effort. And, again, your purpose is instinctual and innate, which means it's something that comes naturally. I reflected back on my life and asked myself, "What I have done instinctively to affect other people?" The answer came quickly: Empowerment. Empowering others to be their best was something I had been doing all of my life, even as a child on the playground. It's what I do almost effortlessly. That was my "aha moment." For years, I discounted it because it seemed too common, but so much fell into place when I acknowledged that empowering others was my true signature and core mission in life.

Next, I listed all of the other hats I wear and gifts I operate in around the wheel, on the "spokes" emanating from the center. These gifts are avenues through which my core gift of empowerment flows. Counseling, teaching, administration, leadership, coaching, and writing are the platforms I have used to achieve the goal of empowering others. Understanding this gave me a sense of freedom because it meant that I didn't have to limit my purpose to one particular job or assignment.

Secondly, your purpose will show up in response to a particular problem, need, or crisis. God gave you your purpose to answer a need or to fit in an empty space that needs to be filled. Where and how do you occupy space on the earth? Your gift carries a solution to a problem that is already present or has yet to arise. For instance, whenever I encounter someone who expresses an inability to do or achieve something, I try to empower them to think and do differently. Think about what you do instinctively in response to a problem or a need. Your answer to this will help you identify your heartbeat, your "center," and will point to who you are and what you do best.

Third, your purpose always produces a specific outcome. This gets to the heart of our purpose and how to identify it. Remember, purpose is your mission. It answers the "what" and "why" in your life. Why do you do what you do? What is the frequent outcome? Each time you operate in your predominant gift, think about what happens as a result. Whatever your answer is, chances are it will be an indication of your purpose and mission in life.

My best friend Myka is creative and crafty. She loves to sew, bake, and decorate. Not only does she love doing it for herself, she absolutely loves to do it for other people. Although she is gifted in other ways, her creative abilities are her dominant gift and the area about which she is the most passionate (I will talk more about passion in the next chapter). One day as we discussed purpose together, she said she didn't think being creative was a big deal.

"I just make pillows and bake for others," she said. "How can something so small be considered my purpose in life?"

So I asked her the "why" question. "*Why* do you do those things? Why do you find them so rewarding?"

Suddenly it was as if a lightbulb appeared over her head. She realized that being creative was more for her than just baking and making pillows and blankets. Her creative gift enabled her to help bring to pass someone's vision for an event or occasion. She enjoys being able to bring ideas to life. The response from her recipients are always the same, gratefulness and joy. *Bingo!* She identified her purpose in life.

So many of us do what Myka was doing. We ignore what makes us great because it appears so small to us. In her eyes her dominant gift was so minuscule and insignificant that she could not perceive how God could use it. But she learned that divine purpose is often found in the most common of places.

YOUR SUCCESS ZONE

Knowing your purpose helps you to create your success zone. These are the areas in your life which enable you to succeed and soar in your work, ministry and relationships. Abundant living begins when you gain a clear understanding of the places in which you thrive. It creates vision and possibilities. Your success zone also includes the areas where you make the greatest impact. God has gifted each of us in a way that enables us to have a deep and profound effect on things and people around us. Purpose always impacts people, systems, and things. Where do you create the most impact? Is it in your relationships? On your job working with systems? Is it in partnership with other people? The moment you discover where you most create an impact, it becomes your job to be intentional and deliberate about creating opportunities to do it more often.

It was only a few years ago that I discovered I make the most impact empowering women. I always seem to generate a significant response when I begin helping women to overcome obstacles and make significant movement toward life change. This knowledge enabled me to walk in purpose daily. With this mindset, I found that I could empower women anywhere, at any time. I could intentionally strike up a conversation with someone who was struggling to overcome life's challenges and offer her words of inspiration. I am now empowering others through my writing and social media connections as well as utilizing my leadership abilities to help women to discover and fulfill their purpose.

When you become aware that you already have what you have been looking to discover, it empowers the "greater you" to come forward. It also releases an authority in you to be the commander of your ship. You no longer have to wait for someone else to hand you the tools or build you a platform to live in your purpose. Because you are aware of what you carry within you, it is now possible to become intentional about creating a platform wherever you are.

SKILL BUILDER

QUESTIONS FOR REFLECTION

1. What are one or two things you do consistently and instinctively, with relative ease and effectiveness?
2. Why do you do it? Why do you find it easy and/or rewarding?
3. What impact does it make?
4. If money were not an issue, what type of career or assignment would make you jump out of bed in the morning?
5. What kinds of people or situations do you feel called to help or impact the most?
6. Think of a situation that seemed to really fit you, one in which you felt you were doing what you were born to do. Describe it.
7. Refer back to Diagram 1 and draw a similar diagram for yourself. What is your center? What skills, and gifts are attached to your center?
8. How can you be more intentional about living in your purpose every day?

CHAPTER 2

Locating the Intensity

—⊗⊗⊗—

"We lose ourselves in the things we love. We find ourselves there too"

(KIRSTIN MARTZ).

HAVE YOU EVER FOUND YOURSELF working on a project only to look up and discover with surprise that hours have gone by instead of minutes? This is what passion will produce: A miniature world in which time and limitations have no place. If you are still wondering about your purpose, just work backwards and discover your passion. Your passion acts like an usher guiding you to the right place. Passion will bring you face to face with the deepest parts of who you are and your God-given mission in life.

Contrary to popular belief, your passion is not the same as your purpose. Passion is the emotional intensity you feel when you are doing something that is deeply fulfilling. The definition of passion is, "the object of an intense interest or enthusiasm."[6]

When you begin excavating your passions, you will also unearth the deepest parts of your emotional being. You will discover the things in life that move you deeply, even to tears, and trouble your heart. You will also encounter those things that create intense feelings of joy, satisfaction, and contentment. If you can locate the sources of such intensity, you will be closer to understanding your purpose.

FINDING YOUR SIGNATURE

Passion extends beyond something you simply like or desire. Passion is far more intense. You can live life and not always indulge in the things you like. You may enjoy chocolate cake, going to the movies, or reading a good book. However, more than likely, you won't feel a huge sense of emptiness if you don't engage in these things. But when you are passionate about something, your heart says, "If I don't engage in this, my life is incomplete." Passion creates a sense of emotional completeness.

A young woman stood up in an empowerment workshop I taught a few years ago. "I have a lot of passions in life," she said. "How do I know which one is connected to my purpose?" This was a great question, one in which many people have a difficult time answering: *How do I align my passions with my purpose in life?* Chances are, you will always have more than one passion in life; but you will probably have one passion that burns brighter than all the others.

I am extremely passionate about singing, traveling, reading, organizing events, image building, fashion—and especially jewelry shopping. However, none of these compare to the emotional and spiritual fulfillment I experience from empowering another woman to overcome her issues and embrace her potential.

Your passion—or what I like to call your *signature* passion—is that thing you do that gets you the most fired up. It is what troubles you and deeply moves your heart and soul. Your signature passion includes things that make you cry or about which you become emotionally disturbed. Even more so, the passions you feel most deeply about are the ones that are connected to a network of meaning.

I was often teased as a child and frequently ostracized by the neighborhood kids. This treatment created such a place of insecurity and inferiority within me that I consistently struggled to believe I had the capacity to do anything well. I had few cheerleaders around me who could help me see beyond my perceived inadequacies. As a result, however, I realized an intense desire in adulthood to become that cheerleader for girls and young women who struggle to overcome the pain of their past and achieve more and become more. While I've always had the gift of empowerment, I didn't become passionate about it until after I went through my own personal pain. Similarly, your signature passion is crafted in the furnace of your affliction, and its intensity is often connected to the depth of your pain.

A painful history, however, is not the only carving tool used to create your signature passion. Your signature passion can be forged as a result of positive experiences that deeply moved or touched your heart. Tanya is an IT specialist who is passionate about building and improving systems. She learned this as a child, watching and helping her father build and rebuild computers. Years later, she became a program developer and consistently rose through the ranks at her job. She shared with me in one of our coaching sessions that those early years of watching her father build computers helped instill in her a passion to develop and build systems that would contribute to a company's overall success. Her closeness to her father translated into a passion for working with computer systems.

Your story may be different from mine. It may be nothing like Tanya's. But you have your own story of how your passion came into being. When you connect to your story, you will connect to your passion. The things you feel most deeply and most intensely about are things that have been embedded in you by God, to impact things larger than you.

PURSUE YOUR PASSION

I grew up in a place and time in which passion was not discussed. We were raised to handle our obligations and duties. We didn't work for enjoyment, we worked out of necessity. Passion had no place. So for years the deeply intense emotional parts of ourselves were not allowed to be explored or expressed. But I believe there are some passions within us that—if we don't act on them—leave huge holes in our souls.

Your soul was created to operate at a level of maximum performance. When you live beneath your soul's capacity, you will become out of balance. You will be frustrated. When your passions are not given a place to grow and mature, you are forced to live a status quo life of predictability. The result, I believe, is that today there is a generation of men and women who have starved their passions and are struggling to find a sense of what really moves and motivates them for success.

Your passions have to be acknowledged if you are ever to get in tune with your capabilities and possess the necessary frame of mind to impact other people. It's almost impossible to discover a passion and not want to share it with someone else. Because passion creates a place of emotional centeredness and fulfillment, it's only natural to want others to feel the same beauty and freedom you feel when you engage in it.

PASSION IS YOUR CONFIRMATION

I am often asked the question, "Which passion should I pursue?"

My answer is always, "All of them."

This answer typically generates confused looks from the other person. I think that is because we have been taught that you can't "have it all." So we think we have to limit ourselves to one—or even none. But I believe that when God created us, He gave certain gifts, talents, proclivities, and passions to enhance our lives (see Ephesians 4:7-8). So if God has placed these things within us, why would He want us to engage in just one? Whatever you are passionate about, that passion is your confirmation that God wants you to pursue it.

The issue, therefore, is not that we have to choose one passion to pursue, but rather knowing the right time in your life to engage in the right passion. Several years ago I had a desire to start a young mothers group for Christian women. I wanted this group to be exciting and active. I created the blueprint, objectives, and even selected individuals to help. But the idea never panned out. Why? Because I was not in the right time of my life to sustain a new program. I was working as an associate pastor at my church, overseeing five programs and personally running two. I was preaching and teaching everywhere, and my daughter had just become a toddler. I was overwhelmed and could not dedicate the time needed to sustain a new team and build the kind of infrastructure that would ensure success. When it failed, I was discouraged and actually threw the idea away. I concluded that leading that group was not a passion I should have pursued. Years later, however, I realized that there was nothing wrong with my passion, but only with my timing.

Timing is important. Your passions can be confirmation of your purpose, but it doesn't necessarily mean you have to—or even should—pursue all your passions simultaneously, with the same intensity.

FAN THE FLAME

I learned years ago that discovering my passion is different than just working on an assignment. Passion can actually keep you in position when you become frustrated in the arena of your assignments. What do I mean by this? Sometimes the constant presence of challenges, obstacles, and frustration in your current assignment can lead you to believe it's a sign that you should do something else. Struggle and stress can stifle the flames of excitement and enthusiasm for what you are doing. But when you are passionate about what you are doing, you will more easily move beyond the frustration and find new ways to manage the existing roadblocks and obstacles in your life.

Your passion will also help you redefine a new path when your current assignment is no longer available to you. Christopher Reeve was a movie and television actor, producer, and director who was best known for his movie portrayal of *Superman*. For many years he was applauded for his acting abilities. But in 1995, a devastating horseback-riding accident paralyzed him from the neck down and prevented him from being able to act in films. Christopher Reeve's "assignment" as an actor was over, but his passion to touch lives was still alive. Reeve became a champion for those who suffered paralysis and other physical challenges; like his Superman character, he fought a real-life battle for "truth and justice" and the rights of others. Christopher Reeve didn't allow his obstacles or limitations to smother his flame or passion for touching others. Instead he found new ways to redefine his life.

Regardless of the obstacles you face, don't allow challenges to change the intensity of your passion. Discover new ways to fan the flame of your passions in order to keep them alive. When you embrace your passion, it will help you redefine new avenues of operating in your purpose.

BREAKING THE MOLD

Living your passion is the ultimate expression of the "greater you." Passionate living will empower you to break free from the mold of expectation that others build around you. When you use passion as a guidepost it will help you distinguish the difference between your **"should-do," "could–do"** and **"expected-to"** roles in life.

People who operate from a **"should-do"** mentality often choose their assignments based on a sense of obligation or duty. For example, the need to become involved in your church or community may be a result of feeling, "I *should do* more to help." The emotional and sometimes financial obligation to help your family and friends who are in need will also create a "should do something" mindset. There is nothing wrong with operating from a "should-do" mindset. Many great philanthropists have changed the future of those who were disadvantaged simply because they felt that they "should do something."

However, if you operate for too long out of what you *should be doing*, you may find yourself feeling over-committed, burnt out, stressed, burdened, and unable to say no because of a sense of guilt and obligation. Doing something just because you "should" will not fill the emotional place in your heart.

Your **"could-dos"** arise out of the need and desire to work in the area of your skill and gift. Those who are multi-talented and gifted in various ways often find themselves simultaneously operating in several different capacities simply because they can. They can be seen as the proverbial "jack of all trades but master at none!" Such people appear highly gifted and talented, while internally they suffer from high stress and no focus. For instance, I have a good friend who is talented in many areas. She sings, styles hair, works as a counselor, sells jewelry, and is also a travel agent. But when I asked, "What is your "signature passion?" she was hard pressed to answer. She "could do" so many things—and *was* doing them, to the point of exhaustion—that she couldn't pinpoint anything as her signature strength and focus.

Operating from what you "could-do" does not lend itself to developing, fine-tuning, and strengthening a signature passion, and thus distracts or prevents you from fully living out your purpose. You can be gifted to do something and simultaneously not be passionate about doing it. Many people have remained stuck in jobs and ministries because they were operating out of their talents and gifts, but not in their passion.

Your **"expected-to"** roles are those you have inherited or adopted due to someone else's expectations. Growing up, I had a friend who was a phenomenal painter. She wanted to major in the arts in college, but was told by her parents that fine art wasn't a practical career choice. Her parents expected her to attend college and find a profession in which she could make money. She did. She obtained a business degree, but continued to paint as a hobby. I saw her a few years ago, and in the course of our conversation she acknowledged that working in the corporate world was never her passion. She said if she could, she would go back and follow her dreams of being an artist, but she felt trapped by her obligations and didn't believe she could start over. I feel great sadness for her. And she is not alone; I have coached women who truly wanted to do something different with their lives, but felt bound to follow the expectations, rules, and traditions of family and friends.

Once you embrace your passion and purpose, you must never allow the opinion of others to determine who you should be, or which direction in life you are expected to pursue. "The greater you" was born without limitations.

Pursuing your passion and purpose means that you will have to break free from the expected norms and patterns to follow a heartbeat that at times, only you and God can hear.

SKILL BUILDER

QUESTIONS FOR REFLECTION

1. What do you daydream about the most?
2. What are you so passionate about that it sometimes brings you to tears?
3. What do you do that is deeply satisfying—something you would love to do more?
4. List the things you feel most passionate about.
5. From the list above, choose one passion that burns brighter than the others.
6. If you were given a million dollars to spend, but could not use it on yourself, what problem would you solve?

Step 2
Authenticate Your Life

CHAPTER 3
Find Your Fit

—⁂—

*"I had no idea that being my authentic self could make me as
rich as I've become. If I had, I'd have done it a lot earlier"*

(OPRAH WINFREY).

A S A FIVE- AND SIX-YEAR-OLD girl I used to sneak into my father's closet and try on his shoes. I loved to clomp around
the house in them, pretending I was going somewhere. I remember carefully maneuvering my feet so that I could make my
way up and down the stairs. At that age, I couldn't understand
why I couldn't fit them. No matter how hard I tried, I couldn't
get my feet to cooperate and grow to his size. My father tried to
explain it to me. "You can't walk in them, because those shoes
were not made for your feet," he said.

Maybe you did something similar as a child. Many people
have. Unfortunately, many adults make the same mistake and
suffer the same misunderstanding. They spend years trying to
walk in someone else's shoes, only to discover later that those
shoes were not made for their feet.

The Bible tells the story of David, a young shepherd boy
whose father sent him to the battlefield to check on his older brothers and deliver food to them. When David arrived,

he found the entire Israelite army—including his brothers—quailing in fear because of a giant Philistine warrior named Goliath who had been taunting them and daring them to send someone out to fight him. David decided to throw his hat in the ring. He offered to fight the intimidating Philistine soldier. But David was no soldier. He had no armor. So King Saul—who must have figured he had nothing to lose by letting the young man try his hand against the enemy—gave his armor to David. Once David was suited up, however, he realized this would not work. The king's armor was not made for him. He had never walked in it, let alone try to fight in it. So he took off the armor, telling Saul, "This doesn't fit me." Instead of armor and a sword, David faced Goliath with a sling and five smooth stones. He ran into battle in his own clothes, with his own weapons, on his own terms.

Your greatest fight may never be with a physical Goliath, but you will constantly have to do battle with forces that threaten to limit the expression of your true gifts, talents, and vision. Discovering "the greater you" requires you to find and embrace your true fit. That true fit is about you embracing all of who you are—those unique gifts, talents, strengths, and purposes and integrating them into the right place and people for them to thrive and grow.

What Is Authenticity?

According to psychologists Michael Kenis and Brian Goldman, authenticity is "the unobstructed operation of one's true or core self in one's daily enterprise."[7] Living authentically is achieving congruence between who you intend to be and who you really are. This requires you to have a strong sense of awareness and knowledge of self.

This can be difficult to achieve when you face competing expectations and perceptions, both from within yourself and from others. After counseling for several years, I found that children are not born with a filter to expressing and revealing their true selves. If you are able to think back to your early childhood, you may remember having a sense of confidence and assurance that it was okay to be you. It is only after consistent rejection, criticism, critique, and abandonment that you developed a sense that being you was *not* okay. Such painful experiences can make you doubt, question, and even change your opinion of your gifts, talents, and self-worth.

Many of us have an internal perception of self and a relational style that was formed (at least in part) by the opinion and viewpoints of family and friends, bullies on the playground, an abusive relationship, or a traumatic experience. In such cases, the task of recognizing "the greater you" is made much more difficult because our self-image was molded or defaced by others. Therefore we often fail to manifest our authentic selves. We become who we *think* others want us to be. Unless we experience deliverance from such negative messages we may have heard or received, we may struggle our entire life, witnessing greatness in others and never living it for ourselves.

SHADOW DWELLERS

My husband Harold is one of the smartest men I know. But for years—in grade school and parts of high school—he was actually ashamed of his intelligence. He learned that being the smartest kid in the class also made you the most unpopular within your peer group. So, in order to fit in with his peer group, he decided to conceal his knowledge and not try to excel. Then one day a classmate received praise for being "so smart." But Harold knew this classmate cheated on every test. His competitive streak won out over his desire to be accepted; he decided to secretly challenge himself to get a higher grade on the next test than that classmate could get, even by cheating. He won his private contest, getting an A on his exam—and in the process learning an important lesson, never to compromise his true self for the sake of fitting in with the crowd.

How often have you felt the pressure to be someone or do something that was just "not you?" Have you ever compromised your integrity to gain a little acceptance or praise? Have you "played dumb" to make others around you more comfortable? Honestly, we probably all have. The pressure to acclimate and assimilate is a cultural norm. You've seen the looks people receive in church, for example, when they are dressed "differently" than everyone else or when they act "weird." We want to act in ways that meet expectations and fit within the comfort level of others. This creates a sense of acceptance and belonging, and much of it is normal—even healthy behavior. Places of employment and many organizations require conformity to certain policies and practices, for good reasons. Conformity in certain circumstances reveals a desire for unity and a willingness to think of others and sacrifice for the good of all.

Conformity becomes a problem, however, when it interferes with your ability to be authentic. When making others comfortable means pretending to be something or someone you're not, then you're not being true to yourself. You've probably felt it before, that feeling of being "out of sync" and out-of-sorts. In spite of how things appear on the surface, something isn't right. It produces a sense of unrest and dissatisfaction that you may not be able to explain. It's a feeling of inauthenticity, when your values, abilities, and preferences no longer match up to who you really are or the people you are connected to.

A good friend of mine calls it being a "Shadow Dweller." Shadow dwellers are women who struggle to embrace their own sense of self. Sometimes it's because the years of rejection, isolation, or abandonment have made them content to dwell in the shadows of life, hiding their gifts, talents, education, and greatness for fear of ridicule and further rejection. Shadow dwellers are waiting for others to recognize how great they are, before they venture out into the light.

I came from a very strong authoritarian household and church, where the value of conformity and following the rules was applauded. I learned early on that it was easier to "go along to get along" than to make waves and create conflict. I carried this same mindset into every subsequent job and relationship. For years I did exactly what people expected of me and tried hard not to go against the grain. After doing this for quite a while, I had no ability to decipher if I was acting in accordance to who I was or what was expected. I lacked self-awareness as to what really mattered to me, what I desired, and where I wanted to go in life. I conformed my dreams and lifestyle to the expectations of whoever my leaders and significant peers were at the time. The benefit for me was that doing this accommodated my conflict-avoidant relational style. Because I got along with everyone, I didn't have to deal with the drama and rejection that went with being different. However, as my external conflict lessened, my internal conflict increased. I was depressed for many years and lost countless nights of sleep over the constant feelings of dissatisfaction with my life. I desired and wanted more, but didn't know what more looked like or how to make it happen.

GREAT AWAKENING

One year in my church's women's ministry, I was asked to teach a series on "The Power to Be Me." How ironic! I had spent much time, energy, and effort trying hard to get as far away from me as I could. But in that small classroom, I finally had to face myself in the mirror. The image staring back at me was an imposter I had created: Smiling when I really wanted to cry, shaking my head yes when I really wanted to say no. I had become the great pretender, acting my way through life and praying no one caught on to my game. I had created a likeable image, one I believed to be rejection-proof. But "The Power to Be Me" class led me to a crossroads: I had to decide if I wanted to play it safe and keep pretending or finally become the woman I was destined to be.

God often uses ironic or paradoxical circumstances to bring you to a place of awakening, places where God reveals that there is a depth of glory in you, much deeper than what is apparent. Beneath whatever façade, position, and title you may have, there is a "greater you" that the world has yet to see and discover. You will never tap into the full wealth of your potential, until you remove the lid that limits the creative expression of all that is true and real about you.

AUTHENTICITY-IT'S PAIN AND POWER

Authenticity comes with its share of risks. I had spent so much time impersonating other people and hiding who I really was, that I didn't have a clue as to how to be genuine. The fear of rejection and criticism haunted me each time I attempted to take off the mask. Becoming aware of yourself doesn't just mean acknowledging your strengths, gifts, talents, and positive traits; it also includes weaknesses, issues, and idiosyncrasies that you would rather forget. For a perfectionist like me, this was the worst part of becoming real. I had to uncover the parts of me, I had taken great pains to beautify and dress up.

A life of authenticity also includes seasons of rejection. Being true to yourself may not be understood or accepted by everyone. In fact, the moment you begin to embrace who you are, you should expect all hell to break loose, especially in your relationships.

Your relationships have been formed around an image of yourself that you have presented to others. So you should expect some painful or difficult adjustments as you learn to be true to you. For example, if you played the part of a people pleaser, you attracted and encouraged people who expected you to bend over backwards for them whenever they requested. But as your self-awareness increases, your relational style will begin to change. You will no longer say "yes" just to get someone's approval. This often results in conflict, tension, and misunderstanding in your relationships. Giving voice to your actual thoughts and opinions, rather than always echoing what you think others want to hear can also go against the grain and result in discomfort and criticism.

At times it may seem as if the risks outweigh the gains of being authentic. You may have discovered that it's often easier to live according to who people expect you to be, than who you *desire* to be. But doing so drains you of the energy you need to intentionally pursue the life for which you were created. Ultimately, it takes much more effort to live out an assignment given to you by people, than to live out an assignment given to you by God. When you act based on expectations and inherited roles, you have to manufacture the qualities that go along with those roles. But when you live based on God's blueprint, you don't have to manufacture or make up anything; you can just *be*.

Your life assignment was tailor-made to fit the core of who you are. This is why I believe you have been operating in aspects of that assignment most of your life. It is so effortless that it feels like breathing to you. When you try to operate in anything other than what you've been built for, you will struggle to succeed. You will not only struggle to succeed, you will most likely fail. Your gifts and life assignment were created to fit together, like a jigsaw puzzle. Looking at the picture on the jigsaw puzzle box gives you a good vision of how the finished product should look. You can have all the right pieces, but if you are looking at the wrong picture, the pieces will never connect the way they should. Similarly, the pieces of your life will never quite come together if you have been trying to build your life around someone else's vision and expectation of you.

When David prepared to fight Goliath, he tried on Saul's armor but soon realized it did not fit. Instead, David used his old trusted sling and five smooth stones. To Saul and his army of men, his weapons would have seemed little and insignificant, but David knew who we was and what he was capable of achieving. He knew the depth of his strengths and being true to that knowledge were the keys to achieving his greatest victory.

If David had given into the pressure to live up to Saul's expectations and perceptions, he would certainly have failed and most assuredly died in battle. But he didn't die; he gained the victory, because he acted in concert with his authentic self. There is a victory attached to your authenticity. There are things in life that you are meant to conquer, but only when the *real* you shows up can you gain access to the victory that awaits you.

Bea-U-tiful

Motivational speaker Mike Robbins wrote a book entitled, *Be Yourself. Everyone Else Is Already Taken*. He says, "Authenticity is a process. It's something that evolves throughout your entire life. We can't become authentic in the same way that we earn a degree or accomplish a goal, it is an ideal and must be practiced daily."[8]

The "Power to Be Me" class I referred to earlier was just the start of my journey towards authenticity. In the beginning, being me felt foreign. So I occasionally reverted to what was comfortable. But the desire to be better and have more compelled me to abandon the pretenses, lies, and disingenuous lifestyle I had become accustomed to in favor of the life I was built for.

I was in a worship service a couple years ago when a minister by the name of Todd Hall pulled me out of the crowd. He said, "God is going to take you all around this world, but you just have to be you!" That one word of encouragement released me from years of self-loathing, people pleasing, and the need to gain everyone's approval.

The world needs *you.* Out of more than seven billion people on the planet, you are the only one who has your unique DNA. Woven within that DNA is a code to unlock your potential for greatness. When you embrace your unique design, your DNA will be left on everything you touch and will confirm to the world that you were *meant* to be here.

LIVE BOLD AND BLOOM

Being authentic requires intentional movement towards a new norm. You have to practice the truth of who you are daily. There are three ways to become authentic in a more intrapersonal way:

Self-awareness and knowledge. This is a critical component to developing emotional intelligence. According to psychologist Daniel Goleman, "emotional intelligence is the ability to understand and manage your emotions without having them swamp you."[9] Having insight into how you are feeling, what you are thinking, and what you are doing will help to build awareness of your personal relational style and how it affects others. Ask yourself what makes you happy, angry, or melancholy. Record on a piece of paper the instances where you felt these emotions. Who do you become around others when you experience certain emotions such as disappointment and anger? Reflect on what creates these experiences and how it impacted your behavior and thoughts. This activity works even better when you learn to practice it in the moment.

Self-awareness also helps you to take inventory of your unique skill sets and core strengths. In the book, *Now Discover Your Strengths*, Marcus Buckingham outlines thirty-eight different skill sets and details how to maximize those strengths in everyday life. This book was instrumental in helping me focus less on trying to improve my weaknesses and instead fine-tune those gifts that will bring me success.

Self-awareness is not only embracing your strengths, but also your weaknesses. Yes, you have flaws. Everybody else does too. Maturity is the ability to look at all of your mistakes, issues, and flaws, and decide that you are not the sum total of them. You may have made mistakes, but you are not *a* mistake. Living authentically means learning to separate your identity from your issues. You don't have to become where you've been. Your past doesn't have to define you, but it *can* help develop a greater awareness of who you could become. You can take all of your experiences and use them to fulfill your purpose. The moment you accept yourself, you also accept every possibility of greatness you have yet to discover.

Embracing your values and how you see the world is an important step in self-awareness. Formerly, whenever I got into a discussion about controversial topics such as politics and religion, I would often go with the flow and reflect the prevailing opinion of the group. But when I started living more authentically, I would silently ask myself, "What do I really think about what is being said right now?" It took a while before I had the confidence to voice my thoughts, but embracing my values and worldview was a crucial step in nurturing self-awareness and authenticity.

Courage and faith. My best friend Melody told me that one day when she was wrestling with the call to authenticity in her life, she sensed God asking her, "Do you have the faith to be you?" It takes faith to learn to operate in a way that you have previously deemed unimportant and insignificant. It requires you to believe that what you possess not only has potential, but is actually necessary in someone else's life.

Courage is not the absence of fear; it is intentional movement in the presence of fear. Courage was one of the qualities David possessed that marked him as exceptional and later enabled him to become Israel's greatest king. He had the faith to believe that God was with him and the courage to face Goliath even though the giant looked bigger than the gift David possessed. Your talent may seem small in comparison to your opportunities, but if you walk in faith and courage you have exactly what you need to prosper.

Instinct. Pastor and television personality T. D. Jakes wrote a book entitled, *Instinct*, in which he says "all of us have internal senses beyond the physical with which we can better determine what's next, what's safe, or even what's right."[10]

David's decision to face Goliath was based on instinct. According to the story, he never received a prophetic word or sign from God to go and fight the giant. Rather, he seemed to have a sense, a gut feeling, that he should fight and that he would gain a victory. There is nothing more authentic than your gut instinct. It's an internal confirmation that is not always based on external factors. If David had relied on Saul's perception of him, or on how the other military men viewed his ability or his weapons of choice, he would have never fought Goliath—and he never would have won. David was successful because he looked within himself and believed in something more.

———— ❧ ————

If you intend to tap into "the greater you," there will be seasons when, in the absence of obvious signs, you will need to follow your instinct. It takes time to learn to trust and embrace that intuitive sense that you're headed in the right direction. You may have to take steps that are unpopular, and uncharted, but just *feel* right to you. When you get into those isolated moments, its okay to tell yourself, "I believe in you."

To foster courage and faith in your intuition, look back over your life and with an authentic eye, think about the moments when you took action because you truly believed in something. Think about the times when you took a risk to do what was in your heart. What was the result? You may think, "The last time I took a risk, things went south." Sometimes the real victory is not seen in the outcome, but in the process you took in order to become an authentic, greater you.

The story of a rabbi named Reb Zuysa illustrates how authenticity is connected to our ultimate destiny. As he lay dying with his disciples surrounding him, he shook with fear at the prospect of death and judgment.

"Master," his disciples asked, "why do you fear God's judgment? You have lived life with the faith of Abraham. You have been as nurturing as Rachel. You have feared the Divine as Moses. Why do you fear judgment?"

Zuysa replied, "When I come before the throne of God, I am not afraid that God will ask, "Why were you not more like Abraham or Moses?" I tremble in terror because I think he will ask me, "Zusya, why were you not more like Zuysa?"[11]

Skill Builder

1. What are some things you have *always* wanted to do, but felt you couldn't?
2. What hinders you most from being real?
3. What would you risk by becoming more authentic?
4. What mask do you wear most often?
5. What messages did you receive from your family, friends, religion, and media about being you?
6. What's one important step you can take to moving closer to becoming a more authentic greater you?

Step 3
Transform Your Perspective

CHAPTER 4

It's *Because* of Your Past

———— ✸ ————

"It's not the past that damages us; it's what we tell ourselves about it"

(Niki Brown).

"**Y**OU HAVE THE EXACT PAST God wants you to have."
I stopped taking notes and looked up at my college professor who made this profound statement. It struck me with potent force and sent me on a journey that forever changed my perspective of my past experiences.

As I have counseled countless men and women over the years, I have found they each had a common goal: The need to escape the pain of the past. We live in a society that has never been good at teaching people how to handle pain and suffering. We have become experts at learning how to suppress our pain, deny its existence, or numb it. In this day of self-help books, therapeutic practices, and mindfulness mediation techniques, there are still many people who are not aware of how their past influences their decision making, relationships, and movement towards their future. A saying I've often heard quoted is "In order to go forward, one must go backward." But ing back to the past can be an extremely painful expe

Most of my clients were reluctant and anxious at the prospect of exploring and revisiting painful moments of their history. Remembering experiences in our lives that caused shame, confusion, and deep wounds is hardly a pleasant process. Worse, unresolved childhood memories can make us question our own purpose and existence. "If God loved me, why would He allow me to experience so much pain? How can I have a purposeful future, when it seems my entire life has been built around hurt, pain, and disappointment?"

I hear such questions often. I have frequently asked God about the purpose of human suffering and even the purpose of own my pain. Trying to discover or recognize "the greater you" among the rubble of a broken life is daunting; it can seem impossible. The past has a way of conditioning us to expect similar patterns in our future: "If it happened before, it will happen again." Many people live life waiting for "the next shoe to drop," for the next unfortunate event to take place. As a result, they try to avoid the past —and any semblance of it—at all cost.

EYES WIDE SHUT

"What's wrong with me?" Terri asked through teary eyes in her first counseling session. As she cried in my office, she recounted every relationship with men and women that ended in heartbreak and disappointment. She is young, intelligent, beautiful, and highly educated, but can't seem to understand why she keeps attracting the same kind of men. It's easy to conclude that she has low self-esteem and needs to love herself more. But as intelligent as Terri is, she is unable to grasp that simple concept and make it a reality. For most of her life she watched her father use drugs and physically abuse her mother.

Her father was in and out of her life; it hurt when he left, but when he returned he brought consistent chaos and confusion to her world. When her father died a few years ago, she thought the pain of an absent and unstable father would go away too.

But her pain did not disappear, it only transferred to each relationship she attempted. By carrying the unresolved issues and hurt into every relationship, she actually re-created the same cycle of drama, disappointment, and pain she grew up with. In fact, to some extent Terri sought counseling not because she wanted to live her purpose as a woman of God, but because she believed counseling would make her more lovable. She believed wholeheartedly that there was something wrong with her and that counseling would give her the fix she needed to attract the kind of man who would finally make her happy. Terri's purpose to be a woman of virtue, grace, and beauty had been distorted by her past hurt.

To know "the greater you," you must become a student of your past. You must go back and study the events of your life and revisit the places that have had the most impact on you. Why? Because when you go back, you will find that the past is the birthing place of how you think and view yourself and others around you. What you believe about yourself has its origin in the negative or positive messages you have received. Additionally, it is a common school of thought in the mental health profession that our sense of self has a lot more to do with environment than genetics. Who you are has been shaped by the kind of home you grew up in (for example, whether you had a two-parent or one-parent household); the economic bracket of your family; negative and positive influences you experienced within your family and outside (social supports, etc.); religious influences (or lack thereof), and the list goes on.

Whether we want to admit it or not, at some point or another in our lives, we became a product of our environment.

Consciously or subconsciously, our past influenced and shaped our internal psychology, theology—and sometimes pathology. Even more important, our past experiences produced in us a mindset that propels us toward a life of success or a pattern of repeating a cycle of pain and frustration.

———— ✸ ————

Through our counseling sessions, Terry began to see the impact her past was having on her relationships. In one session, as she described years of frustration and pain she experienced with each of her dating partners, I asked, "Do you realize that every male you have had a relationship with has been emotionally unavailable to you?"

She blinked at me. A look of recognition and understanding filled her eyes. Tears began to roll down her cheeks. She recounted the years when her father was in and out of her life and when he did visit, he would be drunk, high, or so violent that her mother would have to call the police to remove him from the home. She began to see that her father's absence made her question her sense of self and purpose. She acknowledged that she often asked herself, *If I were worth loving why wasn't I enough for my father to get clean and become a part of my life?* She realized that as a child, she had come to the conclusion that there must be something wrong with her and that was why her father kept his distance from her. This conclusion became her "truth."

As she rehearsed this truth throughout her life, she made it her mission to find a man to validate her worth. But she kept choosing men who were emotionally distant and psychologically abusive, which not only added to her past pain, but also reinforced her belief that there was something wrong with her.

Perception is everything. It is seldom the hurtful event that causes the most damages to us. It is our *interpretation* of the event—what we tell ourselves afterwards—that has the greatest and most harmful affect on our belief system.

Your perception determines your direction. How you perceive yourself has the ability to determine what direction you will take—or allow yourself to be taken—in life. Your life can only follow the direction of your beliefs. If you don't believe that you are significant or worthy, your life will take on the shape and pattern of your thoughts. You will find that everything you engage in—work, relationships, and ministry—will fail to achieve the kind of results, the degree of growth and accomplishment, you strive for. That's because everything you reproduce in life is a reflection of what you believe about yourself.

Your perception also determines your input and output. Because Terry believed she was unlovable, she didn't have the capacity to put into her relationships the boundaries, self-worth, or integrity they needed to be successful. As a result her output was a self-fulfilling prophecy. She experienced more pain, rejection, and abandonment, thus repeatedly confirming her conclusion that she was unworthy.

One problem with perception is that it is often formed from a child's point of view. Most children are unable to view their past pain objectively. Children blame themselves for the abuse, abandonment, or mistreatment they've experienced. At the age of six, Terry didn't have the mental capacity to conclude that she was not to blame for her father's absence and abandonment. As an adult, however, Terry's perception of herself had not matured or progressed past the trauma she experienced at the age of six. She was a grown woman operating with a child's perception.

The negative messages of your past can hold you hostage to a belief system that makes it exceedingly difficult to recognize and embrace your potential. We often look at our future through the lens of our past, which ensures that our future will be no better than our past. We convince ourselves that anything greater is beyond our reach.

—∞∞∞—

I grew up in a musically gifted family. Everyone in my family— and I mean *everyone*—could do something extraordinary on an instrument or with their voice. We also belonged to a church in which musical ability marked a person as significant and important. For a while, I believed I had that gift for singing…until one day several members of my church said, "Niki, everyone in your family is so gifted, what happened to you?"

I was hurt by the comment, of course. I started to critique and analyze whether I really had this "gift." I started to practice incessantly at home, hoping that one day I would be able to belt out a tune as good as my family members and get others to notice how gifted I was. Over time, however, no matter what I tried, I couldn't seem to get the approval I craved from others. I remember asking myself, "What's wrong with me?" After years of feeling passed over and ignored, I came to a painful conclusion that because I could not sing as well as others in my family, I must not be gifted or talented.

In addition to struggling with those feelings of low self-worth, I was often teased in my neighborhood and school because of my hair and complexion. I grew up in an era when skin color and hair texture in the African-American community was an important factor in your acceptance in society. For years, I experienced the discrimination and rejection that went along with being "too dark" and "too skinny," with hair that was "too short." Those early messages fostered a negative self-image and a cycle of self-loathing.

This hurt from my past became a barrier. It blocked me from envisioning myself as any different or greater than the way others viewed me. Plagued with self-doubt and fear, I often questioned my existence and potential to achieve. As a result, I limited myself to pursuing only opportunities or avenues that looked achievable. I rejected anything that appeared challenging or beyond my perceived ability. I nursed excuses for why I couldn't do more. And despite my desire to be successful, I subconsciously engaged in a cycle of self-sabotage that hindered me from being successful in areas I was truly gifted in.

I ran track in high school. I was good at it. In practice, I would often run my best times in the sprints and relays. But for some reason I could never achieve the same results during an actual track meet. I started practicing longer and even took the initiative to practice on the weekends with my father. No matter how hard I worked, however, my performance at track meets was always average…or dismal. After one meet in which I had come in last again, I was feeling extremely discouraged. My coach, John Tull, said to me, "Niki, you are probably one of the fastest runners on this team. You have the potential to surpass even the best runners in this division. The problem is, *you* don't believe it. You didn't lose because others were faster than you; you lost because you don't believe you can win!"

What about you? Have you ever felt that you were close to achieving a victory and crossing the finish line, only to have it escape your grasp? Your ability to live out your God-given potential will always be short-lived if you harbor self-sabotaging thoughts and behavior. Self–sabotage creates future failure, before your efforts have a chance to succeed. It doesn't matter how hard you work or how desperately you yearn for the promise, self-sabotage will ensure defeat before you even get to the starting line. When we allow the events and the interpretations of our past to predict our future, we can only live a life that accommodates what we believe.

HIDING IN PLAIN SIGHT

When the past is allowed to negatively define your image, "the greater you" appears flawed. It's like looking at your reflection through broken or cracked glass. You can only see parts of your existence and the parts you do see appear broken and unusable. Then, because you fear that other people may see your flaws the same way you do, you may have tried to fix or cover up that broken image by overachieving, people-pleasing, and irresponsible living.

As I worked with Terry on this concept, she acknowledged that she had become an "overachiever" in high school and college. She worked hard to build an external image that would prevent anyone from seeing that she was cracked and broken underneath. She worked tirelessly to be the best at everything. She earned the top grades in her class, dated the most popular guys, and strove to get into to the top colleges. When she graduated, she immediately received a lucrative job offer in her field and worked endless hours to get one promotion after another. Most people applauded her and her drive to succeed. But no matter how much she accomplished, she never felt it was good enough. She had to constantly strive for more, fearing that one day people would see her as she saw herself and abandon her like her father had.

Dr. Chris Thurman, in his book, *The Lies We Believe*, says that, "most of our emotional struggles, relationship difficulties, and spiritual setbacks are caused by the lies we tell ourselves."[12] These lies are destructive mental tapes we play over and over until eventually we believe they are true. Once a lie becomes embedded in our psyche as truth, our relational style towards others adjusts to prevent others from seeing what we believe about ourselves. Thus, we spend years trying to hide our inadequacies and issues from the world in the fear that others will abandon or reject us. Believing a lie about yourself will cause you to disqualify the very gifts and talents that qualify you for greatness. You may spend years trying to hide or fix something about yourself that was never broken to begin with.

Discovering "the greater you" requires you to remove the mask of insecurity and fear and fully embrace your authentic self. Living your life as someone or something else benefits no one. You were born to be you. There is a wealth of untapped potential and greatness in you that is meant to be shown to and shared with others. When you hide your flaws, you also cover your potential. Sometimes we look at our past and use it as evidence for why we lack the ability to be successful in a certain areas. But buried within every imperfection in your life is a seed of greatness that is meant to blossom and give new meaning to your purpose.

FIND YOUR PASSION IN YOUR PAST

After months of counseling, Terry started to discover that her past wasn't the issue. Neither was her absent father. The issue was her interpretation of those events. The conclusion that something was wrong with her made her desperate to find something and someone to confirm her value. As soon as she changed her interpretation of the past, she in essence changed her understanding of herself. Her father's absence was not a sign that there was something wrong with her; it simply showed there was something wrong with him. This realization transformed how she presented herself in relationships. It also changed the type of men she attracted. Eventually Terry was able to connect with the right man and has now been happily married for six years.

What would happen if we looked at the past from a new vantage point and sought out a different understanding of it? If we change the interpretation of our past, we will change the interpretation we have of ourselves. To take it further, what if we viewed the past as purposeful instead of a stumbling block or cross we need to bear? What if the past was actually a carving tool designed to shape us into someone who can handle the God-sized assignment that awaits us? I want to challenge you to consider that the past is not an obstacle or hindrance to overcome and get through, but rather an appointed place in time where "the greater you" that could not have been realized otherwise, was born.

Don't misunderstand. I am not suggesting that your past was not painful —even shameful. But you have the *exact* past God wants you to have. How? While the past may contain your deepest fears, inhibitions, and doubts— it holds the seeds of your future greatness. It is the soil in which your purpose and passion took root to grow—and flourish.

Your genius—the creative principle in your life—springs from your pain. Every painful experience was allowed by God to develop the intensity of your passion. The intensity of your passion is a result of the depth of your pain. In other words, your purpose *needed* your pain. Your past enabled you to develop the heart, compassion, and the creative ideas for the people you would reach and the places you would impact. Some of the greatest inventions, ideas, movements, and laws in the history of the world resulted from someone's pain that turned into their passion.

You have the *exact* past God wants you to have. Without it, your purpose and passion have no platform.

YOUR PAST BUILDS YOUR PLATFORM

The story of Joseph is told in the first book of the Bible. Joseph was the eleventh son of the patriarch Jacob, but the first son of Jacob's beloved wife, Rachel (the first ten sons were born to Jacob's first wife, Leah, and the servant girls, Zilpah and Bilhah). When Joseph came along, he was favored by his father Jacob—which became a source of jealousy and contention between Joseph and his brothers.(Genesis 37-45)

As Joseph grew, he began having dreams. Each of his dreams depicted his brothers—and even his parents—bowing down to him. You might think that Joseph would have been smart enough to keep this information to himself. But you would be wrong. He told his brothers about the dreams, which stoked their jealousy until it grew into hatred.

One day Joseph's brothers ganged up on him and tossed him into a pit, and eventually sold him as a slave to a passing party of traders heading to Egypt. In Egypt, Joseph was sold to a man named Potiphar, an official in Pharaoh's palace. There, in spite of his blameless behavior, Joseph was sent to prison. However, he endeared himself to the warden, who entrusted him with great responsibility. Nonetheless, Joseph spent close to fifteen years in that prison with seemingly no hope of getting out.

As the Bible describes it, Joseph's life was a series of ups and downs, a dark season followed by a period of hope, only to turn into another hopeless situation. I imagine there were days in which he wondered if his dreams and hopes would ever be fulfilled. But the Bible uses a telling phrase throughout Joseph's story: "The LORD was with Joseph" (Genesis 39:2, NIV; see also Genesis 39:21, 23, and Acts 7:9).

You can see that the presence of God was with Joseph through every aspect of his journey. He was present with him in the pit. He was with him in the traders' caravan. He was with him in prison. The Lord was not absent when Joseph suffered; He was there in the darkness of his circumstance and was crafting Joseph's future through it all.

Romans 8:28 says that "all things work together for good to them that love God-to them who are called according to his plan" (Romans 8:28). This verse of Scripture reveals an important principle regarding God's loving care of our lives. God allows for every event in your life—positive or negative—to help create and shape the platform needed to propel you into a wonderful future. To be able to see beyond the pain of your past into a reality that God has a greater purpose for you takes faith and requires a true understanding of God's providence.

That truth shines clearly through Joseph's story. After spending years in a dark prison, Joseph was finally released. More than that, he was promoted to second-in-command over all of Egypt. He was in that position when a severe famine in the region drove Joseph's brothers to Egypt (where Joseph's policies had equipped the nation to endure the famine).

Joseph came face-to-face with those who had hated him and tried to destroy him. But instead of taking revenge on them, Joseph said something remarkable to them: "As for you, you meant to harm me, but God intended it for a good purpose, so he could preserve the lives of many people, as you can see this day" (Genesis 50:20, NET Bible).

His past had pointed to and molded his future. He saw God's hand in it all. He understood that he had been sent to Egypt because of the future purpose he would serve, not just for his brothers, but also for the world. Having endured betrayal, abandonment, injustice, and years of disappointment, Joseph was able to look into his history and come to one important conclusion: Everything he had experienced had been designed to build a platform for future greatness.

———— ∞ ————

There is nothing you have experienced that God did not account for in planning your overall mission in life. My former pastor used to say, "God never wastes pain." You don't have to remain bitter or angry at what your enemies have done to you. Use the left over pain, and build yourself a platform. The negative events in your past may have been meant by some to destroy your perception, hopes, and dreams, but they were allowed by God to play a part in forming "the greater you."

We often ask God, "why?" *Why did you let me go through that abuse? The abandonment? The rejection?* But instead of "why," a better question may be "what?" *What purpose did You have in sending me through those difficult seasons in my life? What do You want me to do with what I have been through?*

People express the notion that they have survived and are victorious "in spite of" their past. But every aspect of your past has a purpose, and in God's imagination it plays a part in shaping your future. So it's not *in spite of* but *because of* your past that you have passion, purpose, and a platform for "the greater you" to be revealed.

SKILL BUILDER

QUESTIONS FOR REFLECTION

1. When you look at the painful experiences of your past, what words come to mind?
2. Think back to a painful time or event that happened in your life, what did you tell yourself about it?
3. How do you think your conclusions and interpretations have affected your ability to fulfill your potential?
4. What is one lie about your past you may still be holding on to?
5. What is one positive thing that happened as a result of your past experiences?
6. How can you use your past as part of a platform to contribute to the formation of "the greater you?"

CHAPTER 5

Recovery Without Walls

—— ✺ ——

*"Healing doesn't mean the damage never existed. It
means the damage no longer controls our lives"*

(ANONYMOUS).

THE TERRORIST ATTACKS OF SEPTEMBER 11, 2001, changed the
world. Americans' sense of safety and security was forever
shattered. Many people lived in a state of panic and high alert
for years to come; some still do. The world watched and wondered how the United States would ever recover and dig itself
out of the rubble.

A month after the collapse of the World Trade Center's
"Twin Towers," workers on the site discovered a few green
leaves peeking through the gray concrete and ash. Clearing
the debris, they found a badly injured Callery pear tree. It was
discovered with a blackened trunk and snapped roots. It was a
wonder that it survived, buried under the rubble without a reli-
able source of water.

It was taken to the Arthur Ross Nursery in Van Cortlandt
Park in the Bronx to be restored. Standing only eight feet tall,
its survival seemed unlikely. However, the following spring, a

dove built a nest in its branches and green buds began to appear.–and, with them, hope for a full recovery budded, too.

Recovery is possible, but not easy. It is one thing to look back and understand that the past has helped to shape your passion, but how does one recover from the pain and wounds the past has created? How do you heal from the heartbreak and disappointing relationships that still seem to plague the heart? How can you move into a life filled with purpose and greatness and not allow the past to define and control you?

Years ago when I was seeking God for healing, I would attend women's conferences where speakers would implore participants to "be healed." When I would seek out some of the more spiritual women for help in this area, I was told to "Cry out to God." I was also told, "Seek Him." And "Ask Him to heal you." But I had already been doing those things; I craved step-by-step advice on how to be healed. I longed for someone to tell me how to *live* a recovered life. What exactly does it look like? There is nothing more frustrating than receiving generalized spiritual advice when you need strategies to implement that advice in daily life.

As I continued to struggle and search and navigate the process of healing, I realized that recovery required much more than prayer and quoting Scripture. To recover you must first acknowledge that something was broken. As Paula White said in part of a book title, *You Cannot Conquer What You Will Not Confront.* That phrase says everything about beginning the journey to wholeness. One of the most difficult steps in the healing process is confronting what has been damaged as a result of the past. Especially if you spent years concealing the broken places in your life, lifting the veil and bandages you put over your wound can be as painful as the wound itself.

The moment you uncover what you have been hiding and deal with it, you are acknowledging that the image you have constructed—maybe even thought you perfected—has flaws. You are also acknowledging that the image you have presented to others has been a lie. That hurts!

—⁂—

Recovery requires courage. It takes courage to acknowledge that you don't have it all together and that no matter how wonderful you've become, there is a part of your heart that hasn't been healed. It takes courage to acknowledge how that broken part of you is now sabotaging your search for something greater.

I discovered that to achieve true and lasting healing requires transparency, and vulnerability. These steps may not be sequential in your experience—in fact, you will find that they overlap each other. But I don't believe you can achieve one without the other. True healing and recovery requires us to become honest with ourselves, with others, and most importantly with God.

TRANSPARENCY- LIFE IS NO FAIRY TALE

As Desiree put on the finishing touches of her make-up in the bathroom, she looked at her reflection and sighed. The heavy weight she often felt in her chest was back, making it hard for her to breathe. She wished she was someplace else. She longed to escape the reality: That she was going through a bitter divorce, and had now become a single parent struggling to raise her three children. She imagined being surrounded by people who actually cared, owning her own business, and having a husband who didn't use her as his punching bag whenever he felt like it. The more she thought about it, the more her chest hurt. She felt tears gathering at the corners of her eyes. She quickly wiped them away and silently said, "It's just not fair. I have been a faithful Christian, a loving wife. How can I be going through this?"

Her thoughts were suddenly interrupted as Sister Johnson from the women's ministry came into the ladies restroom.

"Sister Desiree, how is everything? You look wonderful, as usual."

Desiree forced a smile. "Aww, Sister Johnson, thank you! You know me, I got to keep it looking good. I'm doing just fine. God is good!"

"How is your husband, Minister Powell? I haven't seen him in a while."

Desiree worried that her smile faltered. "Doing well, Sister! I will tell him you asked about him."

"Desiree, is it possible for you to come to our women's group next week? We would love to have you share some words of encouragement on purpose and dreams. You know, many of the women in this church look up to you. You always seem to have it together."

"Sure, sure," Desiree answered. "I would love to. Thanks for asking. Let me get back in service and make sure my seat hasn't been taken."

Still smiling, Desiree left the bathroom. Her chest felt even tighter than before.

———— ⊛⊛⊛ ————

It is often hard for women like Desiree to admit that the persona they've presented in public is not the person they know themselves to be in private. It's even harder to be honest about the shortcomings and personal flaws with which they wrestle on a daily basis. Contrary to the popular saying that "beauty is only skin deep," society constantly teaches us something different.

Women feel a subtle but pervasive pressure to live up to a new "superwoman, reality-show housewife" image. It is a pressure to get married, balance children and work, and be spiritually centered, all while looking "fabulous." Meanwhile, internal struggles with jealousy, perfectionism, people-pleasing, anger, insecurity, and a host of other emotional and relational issues can wreak havoc on a woman's psyche. As the demand to "have it all together" continues to intensify, so does the need to hide behind the mask of materialism, accomplishments, work, relationships, and spirituality.

A few years ago, I met a woman at work whom I greatly admired. She was "sharp from head to toe." I don't ever recall her coming in with a hair out of place. Her make-up was always flawless; she dressed in the latest fashion and always projected a strong aura, giving the sense that nothing ever bothered her or knocked her off balance. One day she invited me to lunch and told me she wanted to talk to me about something personal. Up to that point, she had never really discussed her personal life with me or anyone else at work, as far as I knew.

Over lunch that day, she opened up about her family life and a number of difficult things she was experiencing. After being married for several years, she was experiencing extreme marital difficulties with the possibility of divorce looming in the background. She explained that as the "go to" person among her family and friends, she is often called upon to give advice and support, but feels that it is not always reciprocated. I watched in amazement as this "superwoman" opened her heart and cried at how angry it made her to always have to be the "strong one." She was tired of taking care of others while those she sacrificed for turned a blind eye to her struggles and needs.

"Niki, people look at me and say how wonderful I look and how strong I am. They don't know that half the time I have no clue what I am doing or what my next step is going to be."

Ironically, perhaps, this strong woman may never have been stronger than she was in that moment, as she was probably taking one of the greatest risks of her life—the risk of being transparent.

We were created as relational beings. Eve was formed for the purpose of being *with* Adam, not only in tending and tilling the Garden of Eden, but also in bringing to that pristine wilderness an atmosphere of intimacy, connection, relationship, and dialogue. Her power and ability to fulfill her mission relied on the security she felt and the confidence she had to be transparent with Adam. The Bible describes them both as being "naked" and "unashamed" (Genesis 2:25). This nakedness was not just the absence of physical clothes; it also referred to them as being completely transparent with each other. This word, *transparent,* is defined as "able to be seen through; easy to notice and understand; not secretive."[13]

However, when sin entered the garden, that transparency was shattered. The need to hide was born. The Bible says, "Then the eyes of both of them were opened, and they knew that they were naked; and they sewed fig leaves together and made themselves coverings" (Genesis 3:7, NKJV).

Hiding behind fig leaves was their attempt to manufacture their own solution for recovery. Fig leaves not only provided the right size and texture (perhaps) for covering things; they were also an indication that fruitfulness was present. Adam and Eve's strategy was to hide behind a pretense of vitality in order to pretend that nothing was broken.

Ever since, men and women have struggled to live lives of authenticity and transparency with one another. Like our progenitors, we have figured out how to hide what is real and true behind smiles and veils and masks.

Of course, no one likes hearing that transparency is a vehicle for breakthrough and healing. Few people enjoy confessing that their life is paradoxical. You may be super talented, hyper-educated, successful in business, always considered the smart or "strong one," anointed and admired by others, yet depressed, insecure, jealous, broken, and depleted. For some, the need to keep up appearances, especially within the church, seems absolutely necessary to protect themselves from judgment, criticism, or even ostracism. Many women complain that when they've tried to become transparent with other women and even with their leaders, the information was told to others, used against them, "preached on" from the pulpit, and more. Who would invite such things as those?

BEYOND BROKEN REFLECTIONS

Perhaps your experience includes such a time, when the cracks and flaws of your life were exposed and put on public display. The shame and embarrassment of having your issues revealed may have further strengthened your resolve to remain hidden behind your own fig leaves. If so, although you may be successfully hiding your flaws, you are also preventing yourself from getting in position to be healed.

The Bible says that after Adam and Eve fashioned fig leaf overalls for themselves, "The LORD God made garments of skin for Adam and his wife and clothed them" (Genesis 3:21, NIV). In order for God to do that for them, Adam and Eve had to come out of hiding. Moreover, they had to surrender their home-made coverings at some point; they had to get naked again before they could put on the clothes God gave them. Here is an important principle: True recovery requires that we become naked, first with God and then with one another. I have learned that if I have a hard time admitting my mistakes and flaws to others, I am also hiding some aspect of who I am from God.

But here is another important point in scripture: "The LORD God...clothed them." He didn't leave them naked; He gave them a covering that reflected His purpose for their lives, but also maintained the integrity of who they were created to be.

This portion of Scripture shows us an important principle in living a life of honesty and transparency. When we cover our issues, we become a false representation of ourselves. We show people a semblance of who we want to be, not who we really are. When we allow God to cover us with His grace and truth, we show the world that we are flawed, but because of His grace we are still empowered to live a life of purpose and greatness. Living a life of transparency is an opportunity to allow God's grace and truth to cover and overshadow all of your weaknesses, inconsistencies, and mistakes.

In my conversation with my work friend, I asked a pivotal question: "Have you ever told people the truth that you're tired and need help yourself?" She said, "No, I don't think I ever have. I am so used to doing for others and helping them, I just thought they would see what I was going through and realize that I needed a break."

This taught me something profound: We teach people how to treat us and how to perceive of our needs. If you present yourself as the rescuer, the "strong one," or the "go to" person with the all the right answers, that is how others will treat you. For some, being seen as "strong" is a badge of honor. It can be a double-edged sword, however, in that it prevents you from sharing your heart and communicating your needs. When this happens, people will always assume that you don't need any help, and they will continue to dump their needs and issues on you.

Sometimes, however, the opposite happens: You may be pouring out too much of your heart and pain to others. It may come across as attention-seeking. People view you as the victim. They see you as someone who lacks stability and fortitude. This can put you in a situation where you are being controlled and manipulated by others, and you eventually end up being victimized all over again.

When the Bible says, "Confess your sins to each other and pray for each other so that you may be healed" (James 5:16, NIV), it isn't saying to "tell everyone your business." It's important that we learn how to "'fess up," so to speak. If we are going to be open and honest with others, we should do so wisely. We should find spiritually sound people who have the maturity, wisdom, and capacity to handle our issues and needs. If you don't have anyone to "'fess up" to, keep looking. Don't give up. Pray for God to give you or show you a trustworthy, mature soul who can be a "covenant partner" with you.

During my journey to obtain emotional wholeness, I discovered the healing power of covenant partnership. God sent me other women who I learned to trust with my heart. There is a blessing in finding someone of like mind and spirit, with whom you feel comfortable enough to lean on and share your issues. David had Jonathan. Naomi had Ruth. These individuals went through great trials and tribulations, but their survival and recovery had much to do with the presence and support of "a friend who sticks closer than a brother" (Proverbs 18:24, NIV).

If you are going to recover, you must remove the walls of fear over how others will react if you share the broken places of your life. It is the Enemy's intention for us to suffer in silence because he understands the truth of God's word when it says, "They overcame him [Satan] by the blood of the Lamb and by the word of their testimony" (Revelation 12:11, NKJV). Revealing the broken pieces of your heart will put you in a place of healing and breakthrough, especially when you discover someone who shares that same struggle and can help you apply divine strategies, wisdom, or intercession to overcome it.

SHOW ME YOUR SCARS

Transparency is not just about you being open and honest in order to receive help from others. Being transparent with others and telling your story breaks down walls within the church, and also helps unbelievers witness the power of God's grace and favor in your life. This is illustrated in the resurrection of Jesus and his disciple Thomas. Thomas was one of The Twelve, the band of Jesus' closest disciples, who witnessed many of His miracles and teachings. In spite of all he had seen and experienced, however, when his fellow disciples told him after Jesus's death and burial that they had seen Jesus alive, Thomas responded with doubt and unbelief. He said, "Unless I see in His hands the print of the nails, and put my finger into the print of the nails, and put my hand into His side, I will not believe" (John 20:25, NKJV).

So it was that eight days later, the risen Jesus appeared to His followers—including Thomas—He said to Thomas, "Reach your finger here, and look at My hands; and reach your hand here, and put it into My side. Do not be unbelieving, but believing.' And Thomas answered and said to Him, 'My Lord and my God!'" (John 20:27-28, NKJV).

Jesus understood the restoring and healing power that transparency can have on others. His scars were a sign to Thomas that although he had been wounded on the cross, through God's power and mercy He had not only survived it, but had become victorious. Similarly, the scars you bear are not for you. They tell a story to unbelievers about your ability to survive life's challenges. They reveal to others God's power to raise you up and make you victorious too.

Here are some key principles to help you gain the courage to be transparent:

Pray for wisdom. The book of Proverbs in the Bible tells us, "Wisdom is the principal thing; Therefore get wisdom. And in all your getting, get understanding" (Proverbs 4:7, NKJV). So pray for wisdom and understanding. Transparency always come for two reasons: Either to position you for a breakthrough or to position someone else for one. Pray and ask God for wisdom on what to share and who to share it with. Not everyone has your best interests at heart. There are many, however, who are waiting to be inspired and encouraged by your story.

Determine what you need. Before you share your heart and issues with others, decide what you need from them, and do your best to determine if they have the capacity to provide that. A person's title or position is not always the best indicator of an ability and capacity to handle your heart. I often hear women say things like, "Well, he (or she) is a pastor, so I thought he could help me." A title is just a clue; be alert for other clues—such as personality, availability, sensitivity, etc.—that may be stronger indicators. Determine what your present need is—counseling? Mentoring? A listening ear? Advice? Etc.—and then look for those who are most qualified to meet that need.

I believe that lunch with my friend changed her life. She determined what she needed most was a listening ear of a person she could trust. In her journey toward transparency she learned a valuable lesson that she still walks by today, which is that "there are others stronger than me."

Determine What to Reveal. Finally, whether you are sharing your testimony or seeking out help, determine what level of transparency you should provide. Telling someone *everything* about yourself all at once is never beneficial. Transparency should be intentional; it should help to bring healing and recovery to your life or someone else's life. When we share all of our secrets and issues too soon, it can be overwhelming for the other person, and even the wisest and most patient may not know how to process your story, let alone figure out how to help.

Take a moment to think about the parts of your life you want to see healed. Then share some of that—not all—with someone who is qualified and equipped to help you. When you have done that, share a little more. Little by little, you will be amazed at the level of transformation and healing that occurs when you release the burden of pain and allow someone else to help you carry it to—and leave it at—the Master's feet.

Vulnerability-Not Easily Broken

The 9/11 survivor tree I referred to earlier spent ten years in recovery. When its recovery was complete, it was replanted in the same place they had found it—where the attack happened. Returning it to the place where it almost died may seem like a strange thing to do. Surely it made the tree vulnerable and susceptible to future attacks. But this is exactly how God brings our recovery full circle too. Recovery requires that we be authentic, transparent, and vulnerable. Being vulnerable means that we don't wrap protective layers around our lives in anticipation of the next tragedy that might occur.

Often when God heals us, we make a silent commitment to never get hurt that way again. This can be healthy if it steers us away from decisions that could set us back. On the other hand, when your goal is to protect yourself from being hurt again, you will build walls around your heart, preventing others from gaining access and truly knowing who you are.

Until recently, I rarely showed affection or displayed my emotions in public. But this was not always the case. In the second grade, I cried whenever I was frustrated or didn't understand my work in class, which prompted my teacher to send home a letter telling my parents that I was a "crybaby." She also called me a "crybaby" in class—in front of my classmates. I was humiliated and decided—at eight years old—that crying was bad. This was reinforced by the fact that I hardly ever saw my parents cry except in church, which didn't really count because in my tradition, it was understandable to cry every now and then if you "caught the Spirit."

So I came to a firm conviction: Crying in particular and showing emotion in general was a sign of weaknesses. I decided I would *never* let anyone see me cry. My motto in life became "Never let them see you sweat." I stuck to this and worked hard to develop a hard exterior and stoic persona to present to others.

Years later, after I got married, I was determined to stay true to my vow. Being vulnerable and sharing my heart, secret fears, and hurts with another felt like death to me. But as the years progressed it became increasingly difficult, particularly as a good marriage requires a person to be naked and unashamed, as Adam and Eve were before The Fall.

But all of this changed one day, as I was coming home from a church function. Something happened in one of my auxiliary meetings that prompted me to feel rejected, confused, and hurt. As I got closer to home, the tears started to fall. I pulled over into a parking lot to get myself together. I didn't want my husband to know I had been crying. But I sensed the Holy Spirit saying, "Tell him." I chuckled sardonically, wiped my last tear, and responded, "Absolutely not!"

To my relief, I discovered when I entered the house that my husband had all the lights off and was in bed watching TV. I darted into the bathroom to check my eyes, but heard my husband ask, "What's wrong?" I knew then that God was nudging me to become vulnerable.

I answered, "Nothing." I busied myself getting ready for bed.

But my husband didn't let it go. He pressed me, and I finally made the leap, for the first time to open my heart and share. It seemed as if floodgates opened. I cried for hours. I shared with him every hurt I had ever had in my life. And as I poured out my heart about the years of brokenness and pain I had suppressed, I knew that a new woman was emerging from somewhere deep within me.

———— ❧ ————

Since that night, my life has never been the same. Neither was my marriage or any of my other relationships. I realized that crying wasn't my issue. I had cried in secret for years. But letting someone in where they could know my heart and see my weaknesses was my greatest fear. I never wanted to be put in a position of being rejected again—though clearly there was a flaw in my strategy. Hiding and suppressing didn't result in acceptance and respect—but, ironically perhaps, vulnerability did.

That is the essence of vulnerability. It's taking the risk of exposing ourselves and our hearts for the understanding, healing, and fulfillment it brings to us and others. We were created to be naked and unashamed. Therefore we all have a deep longing to be known intimately by someone else. When our hearts are not open to others, we suffer and so do our relationships.

Not everyone is entitled to have access to your heart, however. Vulnerability without wisdom may open the door to more pain and rejection. As women, this has often been our undoing in relationships. We became naked too soon with too many. Wisdom dictates that we don't knowingly put ourselves in the way of people who are emotionally or physically dangerous to us, but rather allow people to earn our confidence and trust.

The day I opened my heart to my husband, I learned I had something powerful and wonderful to offer the world. Yes, I was running the risk of having my husband despise me or deride me as "weak" or "damaged." But I also had the opportunity to allow our relationship to deepen by giving him insight into who I truly was. More importantly, my story touched something in his life and helped him share some parts of his heart that needed healing as well.

FACING OUR FEARS

Intimacy requires vulnerability. Truly connecting with others requires us to give people access. To do this, we must confront those fears that have caused us to put barriers around our lives in the first place.

Fear is often tied to a past event that was hurtful or harmful. One way to face your fear is to change your perspective of that event and look at it from a different angle to see a different outcome.

Replanting the 9/11 tree at Ground Zero was a symbolic statement that although the tree had been damaged, it was not destroyed. The tree survived the event and recovered. Sometimes we give past events in our life too much power. My clients often tell me, "I was destroyed by it," or "It totally messed me up." I encourage them to rethink their perspective of the outcome and take charge of it instead of letting it rule them.

Re-visioning an event that could have destroyed you, but didn't can not only empower you to face your fears; it can enable you to see yourself as more than a victim. Victims believe that their past prevents them from controlling their future. They think that somehow the past has determined and limited their potential of what they can achieve. However, the moment you decide that your past cannot define you or limit your future, you put fear in its proper place. Jesus said, "Fear not them which kill the body, but are not able to kill the soul" (Matthew 10:28, KJV). You may have gone through things that damaged you physically and emotionally, but if you are reading this, it means you survived it…and are on your way to *triumphing over it!*

I would tell myself this when faced with potential rejection. I would remind myself that although rejection hurts my feelings, the truth is: It *cannot* destroy me. And it is up to me whether or not I let it control me. This truth has helped me to embrace people and circumstances that I would have run away from otherwise. Instead, I stare my fear in the face and tell it "I survived it once, I can survive it again!"

—⊶⊷⊷—

In order to confront our fears of the past, we must change our perspective in a way that allows us to see the benefits of where we have been. As the saying goes, "What doesn't kill me only makes me stronger." The 9/11 survivor tree embodies this concept. Not only did it recover, but by 2010 it had grown to a height of over thirty feet—four times its original size! It grew to tower over the rubble, rather than being buried by it. In fact, it is now an inspiring focal point for visitors to the 9/11 Memorial.

Sometimes the most hurtful events you experienced can become catalysts to the most astounding growth and transformation in your life. God uses those experiences to create a platform for us to stand upon. That platform elevates us to a place of visibility, for the world to witness God's grace and mercy in our lives.

You may be wondering as you read this, "So am I supposed to put myself in a place to be hurt and abused?" Absolutely not!

You were not created to be a doormat, nor were you set free in Christ to be ruled over by others; on the contrary, the Bible says "you are a chosen generation, a royal priesthood, a holy nation, His own special people, that you may proclaim the praises of Him who called you out of darkness into His marvelous light" (1 Peter 2:9, NKJV).

However it is also not God's will that you go through life looking over your shoulder in the fear that your past will come and destroy you. You are called to walk with a silent confidence and assurance that because of God's purpose and power that resides in you, nothing can separate you from the love of Christ (see Romans 8:35).

The Bible says, "Perfect love casts out fear" (1 John 4:18, NKJV). You can't truly love someone and simultaneously be afraid of him or her. Recovery means operating out of love, instead of fear. It means no longer building up walls to shield you. It means vulnerably offering parts of ourselves to others so we can love them—and be loved by them—in a way that is truly authentic and genuine. With that kind of authenticity, transparency, and vulnerability, we can then experience the transforming love for which we become greater.

SKILL BUILDER

1. What part of your life is still in need of recovery?
2. Do you have difficulty being open and transparent with others?
3. If so, why?
4. Have you ever been ostracized or made to feel bad for sharing your truth?
5. Do you find it difficult to share your truth or have difficult conversations with others?
6. If so, explain why.
7. With whom have you allowed yourself to be "naked and unashamed?"
8. What was it about that person or that relationship that allowed you to feel safe?
9. List the three people who help you to feel that way.
10. Where in your life do you need to let the self-protective walls down (marriage, friendships, meeting new people, family, etc.)?
11. What's one concrete step you can take to begin the process of tearing down those walls?

Step 4
Harness Your Potential

CHAPTER 6

The Law of Environment

—⊗⊗⊗—

Destiny-oriented people are able to find the launching pad to
their future within the difficulties of their present assignment.

(NIKI BROWN)

O NE DAY WHILE ON VACATION, my husband and I engaged in a
    water-tubing excursion in which we had to get into a large
inner tube and float down a river to our destination. Because
I am not a big fan of water—nor an avid swimmer—I was not
excited about this trip. The weather was "iffy." The river was
often turbulent. At one point, however, the water channeled
into a narrow canal way and what had been an intimidating,
out-of-control river turned into a fast-moving but steady and
controlled body of water. It amazed me that this river, as powerful as it was, could conform itself into a place where its energy
was unabated but harnessed.

You may be gifted, talented, confident, and "centered," but
if you don't know how to harness those things, you will be like a
ship without a sail. You will drift along sometimes without direction or purpose. At other times you will surge ahead, turbulent
and tumultuous, dangerously going everywhere and nowhere

at the same time. Worse, you can even be exploited by others who sense your lack of self-awareness, direction, and purpose.

I have coached women who were living with under-utilized potential simply because they didn't know how to channel and direct their gifts and skills for optimal results. Some people point to their busyness as proof that they are utilizing their potential. But your potential can be misdirected in busyness too. Being busy doesn't mean you are being productive, let alone fulfilling your potential. You can be paddling faster than everyone else and still be going nowhere.

Discovering "the greater you" requires you to narrow down and pinpoint your greatest assets, and begin the task of nurturing, understanding, and maximizing your potential.

Environment is critical to the health and vitality of your future. Your environment is the place where you have the opportunity to grow those seeds of greatness.

In the early years of my married life, I tried my hand at gardening. I had a neighbor whose flower garden was so beautiful that I wanted mine to look the same way. I got the information as to what kind of seeds she had planted and immediately went out and bought the same kind and planted them. I watered those seeds for weeks and kept looking for the flowers to pop up. To my surprise and disappointment those flowers never made their way to the surface. Because I am competitive and didn't want to be outdone by my neighbor, I did it again the following year and experienced the same results. Feeling humbled and frustrated, I went to the neighbor and asked her why it seemed that even though I had the same seeds, my flower bed remained empty. After asking a few exploratory questions she said, "The problem is not in the seeds; your problem is that you are planting the seeds in the wrong time and in the wrong kind of soil." It sounds silly, I know, but I was dumbfounded at the time because I thought seeds could grow anywhere and anytime.

Your environment is key to experiencing enormous growth or disappointing stagnation. Similarly, the seeds of your potential rely on the proper environment and soil in which to grow. In addition, timing is also key. Just as you cannot plant flower seeds in a wintry environment, so you must be careful about timing in sowing the seeds of your potential.

For example, you may have started a business that failed and concluded that you had the wrong business concept. But it is also possible that you had a sound business plan, but planted it at the wrong time. I have learned that you can have the right purpose, right gifting, and right skills, but if you lack the right timing your plans will falter and may fail.

Coming *close* to the right time won't cut it either. You must cultivate an intuition—a sense of discernment—as to God's perfect timing for you to move. This comes through prayer, gaining input from others who have done what you are attempting, and knowing your strengths, weaknesses, opportunities, and threats.

NURTURING YOUR PERCEPTION

Another key ingredient to harnessing your potential is being aware of how your environment affects your perception. I worked as a social worker for many years. Most social workers will tell you that their work environment is not an easy one. It can be emotionally draining, financially unrewarding, and sometimes filled with conflict and tension. I worked for one agency that was extremely controlling and chaotic. When I started there, I was excited and would often stay late and offer a lot of ideas, but after several months I noticed that not only were my ideas being rebuffed, but I was being limited in what I could do to help my program become more successful.

After being in this environment for years, I was exhausted and numb. I started to question who I was and doubt my potential. While I desired and wanted more, I was no longer sure if I had the skill set or ability to achieve more. I concluded that maybe this was the best I could do, so I put my head down and tried to make it work.

As the years progressed, I grew increasingly restless and disheartened. My self-esteem and perception suffered. Eventually, I realized that my potential would never thrive if I remained in this environment. I had to take a risk and move. To do this, I had to work hard at finding myself again and re-embracing the passion that used to keep me motivated. The moment my perception changed as to who I was, and what I had to offer, I was able to gather up the courage to apply to other positions. Almost immediately, God opened up another job opportunity for me to step into.

Your environment can not only hinder your potential, but also affect your perception. A negative environment will impede your ability to envision more for yourself. If you are in a controlling, chaotic, or dysfunctional atmosphere, your vision and ideas will become stagnant. In addition, you may start to associate your identity with where you are. If you are in a broken place, you will start to see yourself as broken. Conversely, if you are in an encouraging, inspiring, and supportive environment, your attitudes and aspirations will more likely grow and thrive.

Your perception is your GPS system in life. Your life can only follow the path of what you believe and think about yourself. Your environment must not distort your perspective; it must accommodate your potential. Harnessing your potential involves making sure your environment aligns with who you are and where you want to go in life. If it does not, it is time for a change.

GROW IN THE DARK

There are times, however, when God uses a negative environment as a tool to refine and mature you. One of the greatest mistakes I made in my journey was not taking advantage of the learning opportunities that challenging seasons presented.

I am a "runner." That is, when times get tough, I run. I quit, shut down, or leave. My focus in challenging seasons is on getting away from the difficulty. As a result, however, I never took the time to hear what God was saying and learn what he was trying to teach me in those seasons. I mistakenly assumed that the difficulty was confirmation that God was no longer "in" my season and therefore it wasn't God's will for me to be there either.

During one season in my life I was working with pregnant and parenting teens. In the beginning I loved it. But as time went on, I grew restless. I started having conflict with my employers and I wanted more money, so I decided to quit. However, no matter how many resumes I circulated, another job opportunity just wouldn't open up for me. I prayed and prayed for God to open another door. When he didn't, I became angry and depressed. I thought, "If I stay depressed long enough, God will get to the point and come rescue me." After three years of throwing a tantrum, being depressed, and God steadfastly remaining quiet, I finally asked Him, "Why am I still here?" He said, "You can't *go* to the next level until you *outgrow* the level you are on now." My unwillingness to grow in my current season hindered my promotion to the season I desired.

I had great potential, but because I didn't know how to grow in a frustrating season, I wasted numerous opportunities to harness my creativity and gifts. I missed moments where I could have matured and developed.

RIn those three years that I spent mad, depressed, shut down, and going through the motions, I could have been learning new skill sets, taking training courses my job offered, or even volunteering for new assignments. But instead, I shut down and refused to grow in the dark.

What I eventually learned is that the season of testing and difficulty is *never* about the test, it's about my *response* to the test. We often dismiss our present assignments, especially those that are challenging, because they don't appear likely to launch us to where we want to go. I have met so many gifted and talented individuals who completely lost their way in life simply because they didn't know how to grow through the frustration. But destiny-oriented people are able to find the launching pad to their future within the difficulty of their present assignment.

Harnessing your potential involves allowing God to take you through the process of cultivating and developing you and your gifts to another level. As He does with a seed in the ground, sometimes God does His best work in the dark. God will take you through seasons that will stretch you beyond your comfort zone, refine your character, sharpen your skill sets, build your endurance, and cultivate your connections with others. While you are going through difficult times, you must trust the One who planted you there. You must trust that although your present assignment and season feels dirty, and looks dirty, it's very likely the *exact* place where God is inviting you to bloom.

So what does growing in the dark look like? How does that help harness your potential? If you are exactly where God wants you to be, but the season and assignment is proving to be difficult, you must ask God the right questions. *Why am I here? What is your will for me? What lesson do you want me to learn? How are you inviting me to grow? How will this help me in my future?* And be patient—and attentive—to listen for the answers.

The second step is to understand that there is greatness and purpose in where you are. God doesn't just use great experiences to tutor and train us for our future. Sometimes He uses difficulty, stress, and struggle to refine us, enhance our vision, clarify our belief systems, and teach us what not to do, and so on. When you are facing these seasons, you will be tempted to believe that where you are is in direct conflict with your dreams and purpose. But God's Word says, "The LORD directs the steps of the godly" (Psalm 37:23, NLT).

Every step you take is a step toward your purpose, a step closer to fulfilling your potential. Even the detours and wrong turns you may have taken are included in that verse above. I believe in God's omniscience; I believe He knew about your best steps *and* your missteps and included them all in His ultimate plan to bring your purpose to pass.

Therefore, although where you are may not be where you want to be, it has *everything* to do with where you are going. It is a designated step toward your future. Your job is to carefully and prayerfully determine how this step you are on will best lead to the next step, and the one after that.

Finally, take a step back and breathe! Taking time daily to practice deep breathing, actually causes you to become present in the moment.

Learning to be present in the moment is important when you have a number of struggles in your life that are competing for attention. We can become so focused on what's not going right and what needs to be fixed, that we miss the opportunities to appreciate what is going well. Mindfulness helps you to refocus your energy so you can listen and get in tune with God and your heart instead of your troubles.

⸎

When I finally submitted to the growth process, God began to mature me in key areas necessary for my next promotion. It seemed tedious, challenging, and full of conflict, but I was exactly where I needed to be, based on where He was sending me.

A few years later, I was offered an opportunity to develop and direct a full counseling program for the community. To make it successful, I had to draw on every skill and experience I had developed up to that point. Today, I often thank God that He didn't give up on me, even when there were times when I felt like giving up on the process.

Your experiences may seem counterproductive, and unlikely to take you where you are trying to go. But just because you can't see the purpose in where you are doesn't mean that God doesn't have one. Even when you don't see the light at the end of the tunnel there is still a light awaiting you. There will come a season in your life when God will allow you to see the synergy between your past and present and how that synergy is propelling you into your future. In the meantime, trust that God has planted you in a place where "the greater you" is developing.

SKILL BUILDER

QUESTIONS FOR REFLECTION

1. Is your present environment enabling your potential to grow or be hindered?
2. If God is using this situation to focus your attention on something, what do you think that "something" might be?
3. What steps could you take to turn this experience into a learning season and cultivate an environment of growth?
4. What do you think God is trying to develop in your vision and character?
5. What can you change about yourself that would make things better?

CHAPTER 7

The Law of Relationship

———∞∞∞———

Two are better than one because they have a good return for their
labor. If either of them falls down, the one can lift up his fellow

(KING SOLOMON).

H OW OFTEN HAVE YOU HEARD the saying, "It's not what you
know, it's who you know?"

I grew up in a small and sheltered environment. Consequently, networking was a foreign concept to me. Everyone
knew each other in my church and community, so there was
no need to meet anyone else. I was in my late thirties before I
truly understood the power of connection.

Your connections create your expansion. That is, who you
connect with determines your ability to expand your opportunities and capacity. When I discovered at the age of nineteen
that I was called into the ministry, I was excited. For years, I
had struggled to understand what value or significance I could
offer the world. Although I was excited, however, I felt lost as to
the type of minister I should become; I had no idea who I was
being called to and what I had to offer. I could count on one
hand the number of female ministers I had been exposed to.

However, I knew deep down that what I had been exposed to was not a pattern I wanted to follow. I had a silent longing and urging to be different.

One of the most important keys in harnessing your potential is being able to get in relationship with people who can help expand your capacity. As women, we tend to be relational. God ordained relationships when he said, "It is not good that man should be alone" (Genesis 2:18, NKJV). He created Eve as a "helper" (in Hebrew, *ezer*), to help expand Adam's capacity and ability to prosper and produce. God commanded Adam to be fruitful and multiply, but he couldn't accomplish that assignment until Eve came along.

There are two truths we can take from this. First, Eve never knew what it meant to be alone. In God's design, Eve was created to be in relationship with other human beings; women have never known any other way (which suggests one explanation for why many women detest the idea of growing old by themselves). Second, God designed and ordained relationships to help us fulfill assignments we couldn't fulfill on our own.

Many people have a "Lone Ranger mentality" when it comes to achieving their purpose. They attempt to implement their dreams and ideas without the help of others. This may be due to insecurity, mistrust, fear, or hurts they have suffered in past relationships. But no matter how capable you may be, there are people who have gifts, skills, and resources that would enable you to move your dream and idea much further along than you can possibly do alone. My former pastor had a wonderful saying: "Favor comes on two feet." In other words, whatever you hope to accomplish, God has someone who can help you achieve it.

While connections can fuel our forward progression, it's almost impossible to move toward your goals and dreams when you are embroiled in difficult relationships. As women we often love hard and sometimes we love wrong. Meaning we pour more energy, effort and time into building the people and relationships around us and receive very little in return.

For some of us, our sense of security is attached to our significant relationships. The condition of a woman's relationship often becomes the benchmark for her sense of identity and self-esteem. If the important relationships in your life have been healthy and positive, your sense of self will probably be positive and strong. However, if you have been plagued with conflict-ridden, toxic connections, it will not only obscure your vision of who you are; it will also derail your efforts to maximize your potential.

THE LAW OF ATTRACTION

In his book, T*he 21 Irrefutable Laws of Leadership,* John Maxwell says that "who you are as a leader will determine who you attract."[14] That is, the type of people who come into your organization is not determined by what you want but by who you are. This leadership principle can be translated into our everyday relationships.

Have you ever noticed that your relationships seem to keep going through the same cycles? Perhaps you meet someone and it begins well but ends with you being hurt, frustrated, or disappointed in the outcome. Perhaps you've had more than your share of drama-filled, chaotic, emotionally-draining relationships. You may have even wondered, *Why do I keep attracting the wrong kind of people in my life?* It's a common and frustrating dilemma for women, especially for those who believe that their education, degree, and status should qualify them to attract a different kind of partner or friend. But your material, educational, and socio-economic status doesn't determine your attraction quotient.

I believe that people who come into your life are attracted to the part of you with which they identify the most. For example, as recorded in the book of Genesis, when Adam awoke to Eve's sudden presence in his life, we get the sense that he was immediately attracted to her. He said, "This is now bone of my bones and flesh of my flesh" (Genesis 2:23, NKJV). Adam did not remark upon the ways this new human differed from him; he was apparently attracted to the ways in which Eve was *like* him. He saw his flesh and bone reflected in her, and was attracted to her. I think we are all like Adam; people will be attracted to the part of you with which they identify the most.

Thus, if you predominantly project your insecurities, you will only attract other insecure people. If you still see yourself as someone who was rejected, abandoned, and abused as a child, you will tend to attract similarly broken, wounded people. If you promote yourself as the "fixer" and "rescuer" among your family and friends, you will attract people who are in need of rescuing! It is not a question of how adequate or lovable you are, but of how you identify and project yourself to others. Do you see yourself as being strong, capable, lovable, and worthy of love? Then you will tend to attract people who mirror what you already believe about yourself.

Your relationships reflect your expectations. What you expect, is what you will come to accept.

FATAL DISTRACTIONS

Most of us at some point or another have been in a relationship that was tense and drama-filled, in which one or both of the people in the relationship were consistently in distress, extremely argumentative, combative, moody, and even physically and/or psychologically abusive. Such conflict-ridden relationships drain your energy, time, and emotional stability.

I call people who seem to produce—and even prefer—this level of conflict in their relationships "high maintenance," people. You must constantly use all of your resources to maintain *their* emotional and physical well-being, even at the expense of your own. The idea of walking away from them may stir up feelings of guilt and fear because "high maintenance" people often do their best to make you feel responsible for their anger. If violence has occurred, it will surface again, no matter how much you try to appease the other person. If you stay in this relationship long enough, you will eventually adjust your expectations and start to believe that you don't deserve anything better.

Being in a relationship with such a person sabotages your ability to nurture your potential and move forward in your dreams. They will rob you of your joy, peace, and vision. If you are currently in this type of relationship, please believe me when I say you *do* deserve more. You were created to be in loving and nurturing relationships. Don't allow guilt, fear, or a sense of loyalty to keep you locked in something that is sabotaging your efforts to move forward. Just because you have known this person for a long time, doesn't obligate you to stay with them. Don't allow yourself to buy into the myth that says "I can fix them." You don't have to settle for what a person "could be" one day, you deserve someone who already is.

The best way to move forward is to completely sever ties with that person, as difficult as that may seem to be. Depending on how difficult the situation is, you may also consider connecting with a professional counselor who can help you navigate your way to freedom.

CONTROLLING FORCES

In most dysfunctional relationships, the need for power and control is usually the underlying motive. Some controlling relationships are characterized by high drama and conflict, but not all. As a result, many controlling relationships can be hard to identify. There are several distinct ways people manipulate others and exert control in their relationships.

The Overbearing Opinion. You have met them. People who seem to have an opinion about everything and everybody. Of course, everyone has opinions; there is nothing wrong with that. The problem arises when a person presents opinion as fact and insists that others see life as they see it and go along with their agenda. This person will become angry when you differ from their viewpoint and will often use criticism or "the silent treatment" to pressure you into agreeing. Relationships such as these will smother your voice and make you question your own truth and viewpoints. You have a right to state your opinion and feelings within a conversation without having to feel threatened by criticism or consequences. If you are in relationship with someone who can't handle your truth, then they are revealing that they can't handle you.

The Victim. You have probably received that phone call at two or three o'clock in the morning, from someone crying hysterically about some life issue. Normally you would feel alarm, but you sigh internally because you've grown tired of talking to this person, who is consistently bemoaning the same situation. Yet as tired as you may be— you feel compelled to help.

She is the victim. She is always struggling and crying about some new catastrophe in her life. She believes that her urgency or issue, should become *your* emergency. From the outset, it's hard to see this person as controlling. It would appear that she really wants and needs your help to overcome her struggles. But underneath the tears and drama is a need to control others. This person manipulates relationships by using her pain to keep you engaged and connected. They believe that their issues will ensure your continual devotion and connection. This will explain why no amount of resources or advice seem to work. They rebuff or sabotage your efforts to help them become more self-sufficient.

Don't misunderstand. I believe these individuals have real difficulties and struggles to overcome. At times, God may even allow you to provide a sense of help and assistance. More often than not, however, you will find it challenging to help a victim. They often cast blame on others and refuse to take ownership for their actions.

These women can become very demanding, angry, passive aggressive, and carry a sense of entitlement. They believe *you* should take responsibility for an issue or problem *they* caused or created.

Sound familiar? You're not alone. I have also been in this type of relationship which is off balanced and very one-sided. It left me feeling drained and depleted of resources, time, and energy.

You may be thinking, *"but this person really needs my help."* Help comes in different ways. Re-assess the kind of help you are providing. Is it truly helping them or making them more dependent on you? Sometimes we inadvertently, make accommodations to allow dysfunctional people to remain comfortable.

It's ok to point people in the right direction or even pray with them and for them. Your ultimate goal is to help their faith and dependence in God to grow. If your efforts are not producing fruit in this individual, it may be time to step back and allow God to move in a different way.

The Gift-Giver. Some people are constantly giving and helping others. For the person on the receiving end, it feels and seems genuine and heartfelt, as if they really want to help and support you and your efforts. But giving and helping is not always the same. In some cases, the giving is not done so much to support you as it is a means to obligate you to the giver. These individuals give gifts to buy your allegiance or hold you hostage in the relationship. One clue that this is happening is when they regularly remind you of all they have done for you and how they have helped you.

The purpose of such reminders, of course, is for you to feel guilty and compelled to stay connected, or give in to their requests, even if you don't want to. Being connected to someone who has a hidden agenda breeds an atmosphere of distrust. The best way to learn if someone is giving or helping for your benefit or for theirs is to assess their reaction the next time you tell them "no." No one likes to hear "no," of course, but people who are giving and helping as a means of control will get inordinately upset and resort to guilt trips when they don't get their way. Remember, real friends love you for who you are and not for what you can do for them.

The Preacher. Sometimes the effort to control is masked by spirituality. I have counseled women who found themselves in extremely compromising and dysfunctional situations because they were told or made to believe that the relationship or connection was "God's will." Most of these women were being controlled by someone they considered a spiritual leader or mentor in their church. It's difficult to discern their control because he or she may have greatly impacted your spiritual growth and healing. They may have been an important presence in your life during difficult seasons. As a result, you may feel a sense of gratitude and loyalty towards them. You may have even said, "If it wasn't for them, I wouldn't be where I am."

There is nothing wrong with having these spiritual giants in our lives. Pastors and spiritual mentors are placed within the church community to not only foster growth, provide encouragement, and counseling on a larger scale, but also on an individual level.

Unfortunately, there are some leaders who understand this and use it to their advantage in order to get people to do what they want. This control can come in the form of spiritual advice they want you to take. They may also have expectations for you to fulfill certain requests or provide a sense of unwavering loyalty to their needs and agendas. Failure to comply may result in you experiencing the silent treatment, criticism, or being ostracized.

Extreme examples are people like Jim Jones and David Koresh, cult leaders who practiced psychological abuse, using intimidation and fear as tactics, equating disobedience to them with disobedience to God. Relationships that use spirituality as a means of control are devastating, because they take advantage of a legitimate desire to please God.

Always remember that God is a loving God. He does not and will not force you to do His will; He invites you. If you feel pressured or forced to do something you don't feel comfortable doing, don't do it. Pray for God to give you wisdom, remembering Proverbs 2:6: "The LORD gives wisdom; From his mouth come knowledge and understanding" (NKJV).

If your relationship with your leader causes feelings of guilt, fear, intimidation, or confusion you may need to re-evaluate it. Make an attempt to have an honest conversation with them about how you are feeling. If this is not possible it might be time to sever ties. If the conflict is with your pastor, this does not mean you should automatically leave your church. That decision must come through prayer. It may just signal the end of the mentoring relationship. Your mentors and leaders have been purposed to bring you to a certain place of maturity and growth. Once you get to that designated place, you may discover that you need a different level of mentoring and help.

Just because they helped you to get where you are, doesn't automatically mean the relationship is destined to last forever. God allows people to enter our lives for a season, reason, or a lifetime. We must be careful that we don't give a lifetime membership to someone who only qualifies for a season.

Finally, remember that your leaders are flesh and blood just like you. They have weaknesses and are prone to making mistakes in judgment and action. Therefore they are not to be idolized but followed, as long as they are following the Holy Spirit.

THE POWER OF PARTNERSHIPS

Your relationships should mirror who you are and where you are trying to go. You want to make sure that you have people in your life who will support and enhance what God has given you and not try to control it. Disengage yourself from relationships that are sabotaging your passions and energy. Nurture and build relationships with people who will add value to your life and not subtract from it.

The right partnerships will cause your reach and sphere of influence to expand beyond your own capabilities. Strong connections expand your vision and help to clarify who you are and how far you can go. When I met my former pastor, I had a very narrow focus and understanding of the world. I saw everything and everyone in black and white. My lens was colorless, and I was judgmental of almost everything and everyone. Some of this was a result of past hurts and some was based on my strict religious upbringing. But my connection with him and the people in my church helped me to break out of the tiny, limiting box I had lived in for so long.

The right person can help you to see new value in aspects of your life you had previously deemed unimportant. They can also help you see where you are failing. I have to credit one of my best friends, Melody, for helping me to see that my Type A personality was a plus when it came to organizing events, but a weakness in relationships, as I could be demanding and controlling. Her courage to confront me helped me to see the impact of my actions and made me commit to doing better.

Your relationships can also expand your influence. John Maxwell stated in his book *Becoming a Person of Influence,* that "if your life in any way connects with other people you are an influencer."[15] It doesn't matter if you are not in a leadership position, if you are engaged with people, you are a person of influence. But how much of an impact are you really making with others? You could be doing great work, but how much of a positive effect are you having with those around you and on your environment? Learning how to impact your environment often comes from the mentorship of someone who has been where you are going. Getting connected with someone who is already successful at what you want to do will not only increase your ability to influence others but will also accelerate the time in which you do it. Being able to learn about future pitfalls without necessarily going through them brings wisdom without the wait. The transference of wisdom from somebody who has "been there" will help you to excel.

YOUR CONNECTIONS BUILD YOUR CURRENCY

Not only does relationship-building expand your influence; it also strengthens your currency. By currency I am referring to your ability to increase your net profit and value. When you are able to connect with someone who has a greater sphere of influence than you do, the potential for reaching a wider audience with your gifts and talents increases. It also increases your ability to enhance your income and business or professional goals.

In 2014, I moved to Lexington, Kentucky. My husband received an offer to be a CEO so we packed up everything to move to a place that was extremely foreign to us. I was nervous. I was unsure how I would make the transition. But I understood the importance of relationships. One of the board members in my husband's new company was Chris Groeber, a top executive in Kentucky. He and I really seemed to connect. He learned about my background as a leader and passion for women, and endeavored to introduce me to as many people as he could.

My relationship with Chris enabled me to connect with other high-level executives and leaders in the city, people I would have never had access to on my own. These opportunities helped to open avenues and doors for me that increased my business brand and gained me far greater exposure for my efforts.

THE POWER OF SELF-PROMOTION

The key to getting connected often rests on your ability to self–promote. In the corporate world, self-promotion is a common practice and essential skill set. But the religious community often views this idea of "marketing" yourself or your ministry negatively. It is seen as self-aggrandizement. It is perceived as pretentious, self-serving, and lacking in humility and faith. For years, I believed this too, so I shied from giving out my business cards unless asked, and would hardly ever tell people about my ministry.

Although the attitude toward self-promotion differs greatly in these two arenas, what is consistent is that women tend to feel less comfortable at self-promotion than men. Whether subtly or overtly, we have been trained to take the back seat, to work hard and wait for promotion to come to us. Of course, for many of us, the promised promotion never came. If it did come, we were often ill-prepared to negotiate, but rather took whatever was handed to us.

Active self-promotion is not pretentious; it reveals your estimate of yourself and your potential. At the heart of self-promotion is the idea of knowing and communicating your value and the importance of your mission and ministry. Knowing what you have to offer and expressing that value in words or actions is an important step in harnessing "the greater you."

The following are some critical steps you can take to become proficient in self-promotion:

Expand your circle. We often limit our network to a fairly tight circle of friends, family, and maybe fellow churchgoers. But sometimes familiarity breeds contempt. That is, the people who are the most familiar with you can become anesthetized to your gifts and talents. Although they love you, they can longer see the extent of your potential the way an outsider would. This is the attitude Jesus reflected when he said, "A prophet is not without honor except in his own country and in his own house" (Matthew 13:57, NKJV). But put yourself in a fresh environment and expose your talents to new people. Volunteer at a local women's group or community organization. Go on a job interview (even if you are not looking) and practice promoting your skills sets. Join a professional organization or a mastermind group. When you expand your circle and meet new people, it will force you to talk about who you are and what you do. In doing this you can make some powerful connections that may launch you into a new sphere of influence.

Extend Your Gifts and Talents: Again, the story of Joseph offers an example of someone (albeit male) who engaged in self-promotion. While serving an unjust and indefinite prison term in Egypt, Joseph connected with two men who had offended the king and been thrown into prison with him: the king's former butler and baker. One evening Joseph noticed they were depressed and offered his assistance. They each recounted that they had experienced a disturbing dream for which they couldn't discern the meaning. Joseph had the gift of interpretation and after hearing their dream gave each man an interpretation. After doing so, Joseph asked that when they were released from prison and restored to the Pharaoh's favor to remember him favorably to the king.

Two years later, Pharaoh had a dream that none of his priests or soothsayers could interpret. But the butler remembered Joseph's gift for interpreting dreams and mentioned him to the king. Joseph was summoned, told the details of Pharaoh's dream, and offered an interpretation that not only impressed Pharaoh, but also saved many lives. In short order, Joseph was released from prison and promoted to second in command of the entire country.

Imagine how difficult it must have been for Joseph, languishing in an Egyptian prison with no prospects for release, let alone for fulfilling his potential. But he nonetheless extended his "business card" to others, offered his services, and even asked for a referral.

When you let others know what you have to offer, and you do it with a pure heart, you are expressing your faith in God and in his willingness to use you to benefit others, just as Joseph did. It is up to God to open doors and arrange things so that those in positions of influence will mention your name. But you have to put yourself out there. You have to let others know of your gifts and talents. You never know when someone will need what you have to offer—and if you don't express faith in your mission and ministry, why should anyone else?

Express your desires and passions. Too often we keep our dreams and ideas to ourselves for fear of rejection, or even sabotage. But expressing your desires is another form of self-promotion because your dream may actually connect with someone else's passion.

A few years ago my husband created a program for his non-profit organization called Future Leaders of America. His goal was to train inner city teens in Camden, New Jersey, to work in the healthcare field. He tried every avenue he could to make the right connections but for years the program remained grounded. Then one day he got into a casual conversation with an executive in a hospital and mentioned his idea. This executive became so excited because he had the same desire and even had access to funding. He just didn't have anyone to organize it! Of course, my husband was floored. Who knew that a casual conversation could produce such a moment of destiny? Before long they were collaborating and launching Future Leaders of America, with great success.

———— ∞ ————

You don't have to wait for someone to promote you. Promote what's in you and your connections will follow. Your dreams and passions will begin to materialize. When you get into conversations with people, reveal "the greater you." Most people would love to hear what is in your heart. And they may know someone (or know someone who knows someone) who can give you the boost you need to overcome a struggle or launch into new orbits.

Harnessing your potential always involves relationship-building. When you connect with someone who has a passion for where you are going, they can help expand your reach to beyond your own capacity and get you that much closer to receiving the more you desire.

SKILL BUILDER

1. On a separate sheet of paper, list the significant relationships in your life (both positive and negative).
2. Put a star or asterisk (*) next to the names of those people who have *enhanced* you and your capacity in your journey.
3. Put a dash (-) next to the names of those who have hindered or diminished you and your ability to reach your goals.
4. Highlight or circle the relationships that you think are a true reflection of who you are and what you value.
5. What part have you been playing in maintaining the relationships that don't enhance you?
6. What steps can you take to widen your circle of influence?
7. In what area do you need a greater sense of influence and exposure?
8. What is the single most important step you can make to promote yourself, your mission, and your ministry?

CHAPTER 8

The Law of Process

———— ◦◦◦◦ ————

"If you are still waiting, it's only a sign that God is still working"

(UNKNOWN).

I USED TO COLLECT CATERPILLARS as a child. They fascinated me. All of my friends and family thought I was gross. But there was something about them that I found simultaneously beautiful and sad. Watching them crawl through the dirt, knowing they were meant to fly, always made me want to rescue them and help them become butterflies. I would bring them into the house, put them in a jar with holes in the lid, and anxiously wait for their change. But I didn't understand how long it takes for a caterpillar to go through its metamorphosis. So I was impatient. I would become frustrated, take them back outside, and release them. Little did I know that if I had waited out the process, I could have witnessed a powerful transformation and depiction of one of life's best lessons: "Good things come to those who wait."

Have you ever released a dream or let go of an idea because it took too long to develop into what you desired? It seems that time always becomes an issue when you are carrying big ideas inside you. The moment you become committed to pursuing your passions, you will become acutely aware of how little time you have to get it all done. But living with intentional greatness demands that we go through the process of growth and transformation.

Waiting is not always easy, of course. The pleasure of embracing your purpose is always followed by the pressure to make it happen quickly—especially if you embrace those dreams late in life. You'll start analyzing your age and stage of life and wonder if you'll have strength (or teeth) left to enjoy the dream when it actually comes to fruition.

I am convinced that God is often more concerned with *where* you are than with how much time has passed in your life. That is, God is invested in your mental and spiritual health more than your physical location. How many steps of maturity and growth are between where you are and where you want to be? What heart changes need to take place in order for you to accommodate what's coming?

The truth is, time is not really the issue. It's what happens in time. It's the process of waiting through events such as sickness, divorce, unemployment, and wayward children that creates the tension and urgency to move more quickly. When you're unsatisfied, you will tend to neglect where you are and focus your energy on trying to get into the next moment. This can cause frustration because it will seem no matter how hard you try, the further you feel from your destiny.

But often the place you are trying to get away from is the place in which God wants to meet you and use you. We want to abandon difficult places because it feels like they're not getting us where we want to go. But when you pour energy into the present, it builds momentum to propel you into your future.

RUNWAY READY

A few years ago when I was working as an associate pastor I became immensely frustrated. It seemed that no matter how much effort I put into my assignments, the ministries were not taking off the way I envisioned. Like most leaders, I truly desired to see the organizations and programs I was entrusted with become successful and vibrant. I started to feel helpless and convinced myself that maybe there was something wrong with me and my approach. So I tried another tactic. I built up the teams, did more leadership training, created more programs, and whatever else I could think of doing. I eventually reached a point of exhaustion, then despondency. One day as I was crying and throwing a pity-party for myself, telling God how it seemed that nothing I had put into place was launching, I sensed Him saying, "I never intended those things to be launched; they were built to launch you!"

That took me aback, of course, and spoke to me on many levels. First, it reminded me that I didn't build anything; in the end, they were designed for God's purpose. Secondly, it opened up my soul to a new truth, that sometimes the things you are attached to were never designed to be a success but to make *you* a success.

We often connect ourselves to assignments (and even people) that look like they can be the vehicle to our dreams. We get a job that is promising, we are promoted to a new position, or we meet someone who seems exactly what we are looking for in a mate. But when the job, position, or relationship flounders or fails to move in the direction (or at the speed) we hoped it would, we panic. We question if this was really God's plan. We doubt ourselves—our ability, our purpose, our mission, our direction. But there will be seasons in your life in which God connects you to something or someone not because it was a landing strip, but because it was a launching pad, designed to prepare you for your next level.

PLATFORMS AND VEHICLES

If you are going to manage your way through the process of embracing "the greater you," you must be able to look at the various connections you make and the opportunities you face along the way and to determine which ones are platforms and which will become vehicles. We often confuse the two. But there is a difference.

Platforms give us support to stand on. They are those assignments in your life that foster your growth in character and refine those areas of your faith and spiritual walk that need to be matured. For example, my job as an associate pastor in my former church was a platform God used to develop and refine me as a leader and speaker, as well as to fine tune my vision for women's ministries. I viewed my position as a place where God was planting me; God had a bigger plan.

This holds true for relationships as well. Some people were given to you to be the scaffolding in your life. They were sent to build your integrity, vision, character, and faith. For instance, you may look back on romantic relationships you believed at the time to be "the one," but instead they were catalysts for self-understanding and growth, to help you overcome insecurities or redefine what you need and deserve in a mate.

Unfortunately, good platforms often look like fancy aircrafts. They look like they can fly, when they were not designed to leave the ground. We may expend much time, effort, and money in getting them off the ground, but fail in the end. That is because we are attempting to transform a platform into a vehicle. Platforms are never designed to move you into your destiny. They are used by God to sustain and support you where you are.

Recognizing this and making the transition away from a platform is hard because they supported you. When it's time to shift into something new, the fear of letting go of a comfortable support system will entice you to hold onto something or someplace God is trying to move you away from.

When my husband received the offer to become a CEO in Kentucky, I doubted that God was moving us. My doubt was not because I had heard from God, but I just couldn't fathom leaving a place and relationships that had been a support to me for over twenty years and walk into unknown territory. I had become a well-known speaker in that area, and had just started Purpose by Design workshops and classes that seemed to be gaining momentum. Why would God move me now? I was afraid of having to meet new people and re-establish myself and my ministry. What if they didn't like me? Who was going to help and support me in this new place? How would I make my way in this new environment? The truth was, I had grown comfortable and complacent, and that hindered my ability to see the signs and move forward in faith.

Sometimes your support system can handicap your faith. You can rely so much on the presence and help you receive from others that your "faith muscles" weaken. If where you are doesn't challenge your vision, or require any faith, you have probably outgrown that place, and that level. On the other hand, being terrified by your next move is a possible sign that God is inviting you to enter a new dimension of faith.

It's important not to create a permanent season out of a temporary process. The places and people who have intersected with your life may have been just a part of God's plan, a platform to prepare you for something greater.

While platforms support us, vehicles advance us. God often uses paradoxical methods to move us forward. Right before my husband received the new job offer, our family had been in the midst of a severe financial crisis. Harold was the principle breadwinner in the family, but had lost his job the year prior. Although I had my position at the church, it was only on a part-time basis. In the beginning we were not concerned. We each had our master's degree in our chosen field and tons of experience. We were confident that one of us would secure a place of employment quickly.

As the weeks rolled into months, however, our confidence and faith started to waver. Eventually, our unemployment payments ended. In a span of six months, we went from making six figures to living on food stamps. To say we were nervous is an understatement. We were afraid!

It seemed that no amount of praying and fasting could end the season soon enough. We were unclear of our next steps and had no idea of how it would end. All we could do is hold on to one another and God's promise for our lives.

What we didn't know is that God was working behind the scenes. He was using this financial famine as a vehicle to move us to the next level. While Kentucky was not on our list of places to move to, it was a part of God's plan.

We often expect our vehicles of destiny to come in the form of opportunities and promotion. But sometimes your season of advancement shows up in the form of your worst opposition. God uses difficult circumstances to push you closer to the promise. He will move you out of your comfort zone, take away what you relied on, just to give you more! Before you curse and bemoan your season of difficulty—make sure it's not the vehicle taking you towards breakthrough.

To experience the more that we desperately desire, we must allow the process to do a complete work in our lives. To refine us, mature us, and move us to the place we have been destined to succeed. The following are some steps to take in order to benefit from the process:

Define your platforms and vehicles. Harnessing your potential will require you to take a step back and evaluate where you are in the process. Determine if this is a season of preparation or a time of momentum and movement. Assess your connections and location by looking at what and who you're connected to, and decide if this place is allowing you to realize your dreams or is supporting you until the dream comes to pass.

Dare not to compare. It is easy to fall into the comparison trap. When you look at others who are more successful or further along than you are, you may question and even critique the path you are on. *What am I doing wrong? Why can't that be me? When will it be my turn?* Comparison can be great as a frame of reference, but it is detrimental for assessing your value or sense of success.

Comparison often leads to emulation, which can be dangerous. You try to emulate what someone else has done to receive or achieve what they have. This is exhausting and fruitless. To receive exactly what someone else has, you have to go through exactly what they have experienced. Furthermore, you may be comparing your process to someone else's promise. In other words, you may be measuring yourself against someone who has already completed the journey of growth that you are currently on.

Your process is unique to you. God wants to use *you*, not a cheap imitation of someone else. He wants to refine you and do something original and creative based on your personality, background, capacity, and dream He has for you. So instead of making comparisons, promote your uniqueness.

Recalculate the distance to destiny. Corporations often determine where they are in relation to their goals by doing a gap analysis, which measures the "gap" between the goal and its fulfillment. We can do the same with our goals and dreams. At times we look at the gap as a delay. But from Heaven's perspective the gap is a space designed for you to prepare yourself for the future. At other times, however, the gap is not real, only perceived. That is, the distance to destiny is not always as long as we think it is. When we compare ourselves to others and allow our frustrations to influence our vision, it can create a gap where there was none or widen a space that should be quickly traversed.

An example of this is found in the Old Testament when God delivered the Children of Israel out of Egypt. His intention was to take them into the Promised Land. A map reveals that it should have taken them no more than two weeks to get to the land of Canaan. But of course the Biblical accounts reveal that it took forty years. Why so long? Because they consistently complained about the process and allowed doubt and fear to extend their season. What was supposed to be a two-week journey turned into forty years of wandering and waiting.

You may have to turn on your spiritual GPS system to know where you are in the process. You are probably closer than you think. Trying to understand and second-guess the roadmap to

God's promise can lead to doubt and delay. As Isaiah 55:8 says, "For My thoughts are not your thoughts, Nor are your ways My ways, says the Lord" (NKJV). You may not be able to figure out God's process, why it seems to be taking so long, or why He's using one method instead of another, but one thing is for sure: He *will* bring you to the destination.

Sticking with the process is one of the most crucial steps you can take in developing "the greater you." Every step brings you closer to embracing what you desire. It doesn't really matter how you begin or what you have to endure; what matters is what you receive from the journey. That is what qualifies you to step with confidence into your future.

SKILL BUILDER

1. Have you ever given up a dream or idea due to discouragement with the process? If so, write down those abandoned dreams or ideas on a separate sheet of paper.
2. Are you still passionate about those things?
3. If so what would it take to begin pursuing them again?
4. What steps can you take to stay encouraged in the process?
5. Think about where you are currently. Is it a platform... or a vehicle?

Section Two
Embrace "The Greater You"

Step 5
Prioritize You

CHAPTER 9

Prioritize Your Assignments

———— ✂️ ————

"If you don't prioritize your life, someone else will"

(GREG MCKEOWN).

"SURE I CAN SQUEEZE YOU in for tomorrow," I replied to a client who had called requesting an "emergency" appointment. I hung up the phone and sighed. I had just committed myself to something else, one more thing I didn't have the time or energy to do.

Sound familiar? How often have you found yourself saying yes to something even though everything inside of you screamed, "No?" How many times have you gone to bed physically and emotionally drained, but with no tangible evidence of having achieved anything? How often have you put *your* life on hold to help, support, and develop someone else's dream, only to realize later that your dreams were still languishing?

The women I have coached come from all walks of life and socio-economic levels and each of them had something in common: The pressure to please and live up to everyone's expectations except their own. I have worked with women who were extremely intelligent and held high positions, yet felt trapped by the competing demands of work, motherhood, friendship, family, and ministry. All their responses and complaints sounded the same, echoing a claustrophobic feeling, a sense of being trapped in a relationship or assignment they had no power to change. Each had also suffered the physical and emotional consequences of being stretched too thin: Anxiety, weight loss or weight gain, hair loss, mood swings, depression, and despondency.

Why do we do this? What causes us to sacrifice our power and smother our dreams and potential to serve others? Is it because we are women that we are expected to do more and be more? Is it because we have bought into a societal notion that we are the better "nurturers," communicators, organizers, and hostesses? We know, of course, that at times the need to fill multiple roles is real and necessary. The single parent often has to be mom *and* dad, while juggling jobs, finances, schedules, and more. This can also be the case for the woman who is married, but has to carry all of the household burdens because her husband is unavailable (for any number of reasons). Single women are not exempt, either. One of my best friends complains about always doing things for everyone else and never having time for herself; yet on those rare occasion when she takes time for herself, she feels guilty and selfish.

In Greg McKeon's book, *Essentialism: The Disciplined Pursuit of Less*, he says that "once you give yourself permission to stop trying to do it all, to stop saying yes to everyone, can you make your highest contribution towards the things that really matter."[16] Embracing the "greater you," requires a deliberate strategy to pour your best focus, time, and efforts into what you choose to be essential in your life. But how do we choose what's important and essential? Isn't everything important? The answer is no. But it is important to explore why we tend to think and act as though it is.

SEDUCTION OF AFFIRMATION

When I was asked to become the pastor of family ministries in my former church, I was honored and excited at the prospect of being able to do more. The church had grown to what some would consider a mega-church. The church's leadership was high-functioning and fast-paced. Working hard was rewarded and applauded. I jumped right in with both feet. My daughter was a toddler and my husband was working long hours, but I felt up to the challenge.

In the beginning, the position was limited, but as time went on, it expanded from just overseeing ministry leaders to directing several of them. I loved every minute of it—so much so, in fact, that each year I added onto my job description and developed still more ideas and new programs to incorporate into the ministry. Simultaneously, I was being invited to more speaking engagements and events. On the outside, I looked competent and productive. I prided myself on being able to juggle multiple tasks. But internally, I was beginning to crumble. It didn't happen all at once. But slowly and steadily, my busyness began to chip away at my energy, passion, and focus.

I hit rock bottom one morning when I was getting my daughter dressed for school and realized she had absolutely nothing clean to wear. In the corner of her room was at least two weeks' worth of dirty clothes. The moment I flipped her undergarments inside out to make them appear clean, I realized it was symbolic of my life and that something needed to change.

That was easier said than done, of course. I discovered that being busy was an addiction for me. Working in an environment that applauded production only fueled this addiction and made it more difficult to walk away. But life is a series of tradeoffs. In other words, we don't engage in any behavior without believing that there will be some kind of benefit. My busyness affirmed a part of me that felt lacking. There was a deep need to feel and be seen as adequate and significant. Saying yes made me feel wanted and accepted.

———— ❦ ————

Affirmation is seductive. We often connect ourselves to the things that confirm our strengths. We pour our passion into areas that affirm our identities and abilities. At the same time, we will neglect the places that challenge us and don't offer immediate (or at least quick) gratification. It's rare to find a work or ministry environment that truly affirms who we are rather than what we do. Therefore the pull to do more in order to gain greater acknowledgment is strong (though often subconscious). We may not consciously sign up for things because we want to be affirmed or applauded, but our need is revealed when we let a relative or one of our leaders down and subsequently feel guilty or worried about how they may perceive us. *Will they still affirm me and see me as being valuable part of the team?*

If you are in a subordinate position, there is the persistent fear of being penalized or treated differently by your leader if you don't submit to their requests. This fear may be even more pronounced if a colleague or family member is involved; we worry that the disappointment may change the relationship. So we say yes in order to hold onto the relationship, to avoid conflict and, we think, possible abandonment.

Included in our fears is the sense that saying no makes you different. It makes you a non-conformist. Who wants to be the odd man or woman out? The need to conform is real and deeply ingrained. Most of our societal norms and practices are built on conformity. Our relationships often rely on conformity. We become what others need us to be and in return we gain their love and support.

FEIGNED HELPLESSNESS

By the time I came to the awareness that I was an approval seeker, I felt completely helpless to change it. I was already committed to a multitude of projects and clients. I was leading teams of people and had not invested time in training anyone to take my place. My desire to remain in the favor of my leaders became an everyday goal. I felt I had no choice but to be consistently available. I felt stuck, which led to feelings of anger, resentment, and passive-aggressive behaviors.

However, my anger at others was grossly misplaced. The responsibility was mine; I had given away my power to choose. McKeon says that "when we don't purposefully and deliberately choose where to focus our energies and time, other people–our bosses, our colleagues, our clients and even our families–will choose for us."[17] Because of my insatiable need to be affirmed and applauded, I sacrificed my right to choose my path. In sacrificing my rights, I worked for others and what suited them instead of working for what best suited me.

You may not be quite where I was. Your need for affirmation may not be the reason for your over-extended schedule. But if you are overcommitted, there is a reason for it. And a feeling of helplessness may be a factor in keeping you stuck there.

When you are in a cycle of consistent giving with little return, your mind will convince you that this is your only option. It should be just the opposite. When we don't see the fruits of our labor, our minds should look for a way to find more gratification. Unfortunately, we are trained to think in black or white. We will either keep doing more of the same thing to get more results or we will become despondent and give up. There is seldom any gray area or out-of-the-box thinking.

I have often heard my clients express this feeling of helplessness. They say, "I don't have a choice," or "I *have* to do this."

This belief keeps them stuck in a cycle of limited options. They truly believe there are no other avenues for them but to do what was being asked or assigned.

How do we get unstuck? Is it possible to change a pattern of behavior that is so ingrained? Can we start saying "no" now, when we have made a habit of saying "yes?" We can. But it will take renewed focus, courage, and the intentional pursuit to become a "greater you."

YOU HAVE A CHOICE

As I spent years counseling those women on how to take back their power, I was also counseling myself. I too believed that I *had* to do what others asked and expected of me "or else." I could not have defined what "or else" meant but I wasn't courageous enough to find out. My turning point came in a conversation with my older brother Ronald. I was bemoaning the fact that I felt stuck and hindered in my current position and really didn't see any choices. In reality, I had a ton of choices; I was just afraid that if I went against the grain, I would squander the potential to be successful. I hid behind the lie that my success was attached to certain people and fulfilling what they expected of me.

This made me a victim. On some level there are benefits to being a victim. You don't have to take responsibilities for the risks. You don't have to worry about the consequences of disappointing others. You can avoid the conflict and backlash that might come with saying no to people. You don't have to take ownership of the unknown. You can hide behind what "others" won't let you do rather than taking responsibility for your own dream and desires.

My brother finally interrupted my pity party. "Your success," he said, "is not dependent on what organization you are connected with or whose expectation you are living up to. Your success is tied into who *you* are. You carry your success wherever you go."

This was an "aha" moment for me, signaling that I really did have a choice in my destiny. I had the power to decide what success meant to me. Did it really mean working long hours every day, accepting every request, and juggling multiple assignments with minimal results? I concluded that it did not. I decided that success meant rediscovering what I was most passionate about and pouring my *best* energy and resources into that.

BUILDING VISION WITH BROKEN PIECES

The Bible says, "Where there is no vision, the people perish" (Proverbs 29:18, KJV). Vision extends the life expectancy of leaders and their dreams. Vision is one of the variables in our lives that cannot remain static. Vision helps maintain the energy your passion feeds on. Your vision needs to be singular yet dynamic. This means adjusting your lens to block out everything that is crowding your environment and re-focusing on the one thing that is at the center of your core.

A few years ago while teaching a workshop for my women's department, I did an activity to illustrate a way to gain clarity of vision. I selected two participants and blindfolded one of them. Without showing her the box top of the original puzzle, she had to put the scattered pieces together by listening to the instructions of the other volunteer. To further punctuate the lesson, and to create distraction, I asked the class to make background noise during the activity. However in spite of the confusion, lack of vision and noise, the two volunteers worked swiftly and connected the pieces of the puzzle together.

There was a greater message in the activity. When you are trying to get a vision of who you are and your future, it can feel like putting together a puzzle blindfolded. The pieces seem scattered and broken with no clear connection. You are in the dark as to which direction you should take. The background noise in your life acts a consistent distraction and hinders you from focusing on what's important. You have voices coming from different people who may or may not be steering you in the right direction.

However the blindfolded participant was able to assemble the puzzle because she blocked out the external elements distracting her and shifted her focus onto the voice and instruction of her partner. She was able to see more clearly by listening more intently to the one voice that mattered.

To prioritize your life you must block out the noise around you and focus on what you have been hearing. What sound is your future making? What instructions have you been given on how to build the next phase of your life? If you haven't been given any instructions yet, keep seeking and listening. The vision may seem disconnected and scattered but God is your partner. The moment you tune in to His voice, you will gain clarity on how to build with broken pieces.

CREATE CLARITY

With all the competing demands that come to us in the course of a day—or a lifetime—how do we gain the clarity we need? Clarifying your vision involves looking backward, inward, and forward. You have to use hindsight, insight, and foresight to get a good sense of what's truly and enduringly important.

Hindsight. Look back at the steps you took that brought you to where you are now. Were those the right steps? Were there missteps along the way? Were there things you could have or should have done differently? Evaluate how dynamic and innovative you have become. Where have you grown? How have you changed? What have you done in the past that is no longer necessary today? Hindsight is looking back at successes and failures and evaluating them in light of where you are trying to go. Are you still making the same mistakes? Have you lost focus? How have your goals changed?

Insight. Next, focus on what's happening now. Where are you? Are you exactly where you expected to be at this stage of your life? Are you realizing your dreams and ambitions? Revisit the "what" and "why" of your work. What are you doing? Why are you doing it? What is the focus of your desire? What is that deep burning mission and calling that keeps you awake at night? Why did you get into this path or line of work? What are you hoping to accomplish? All of these questions point you back to your center. What you're doing should be in alignment with your core passion, purpose, and strengths.

When you have a clear internal vision of your purpose, it becomes easy to focus on the things in which you should be investing your time and energy. I am not suggesting you neglect everything else you are doing. You may still have to carry some ongoing personal and professional responsibilities. But it's important to evaluate every assignment and opportunity to determine whether or not it is in alignment with your ultimate goals and purpose

Foresight. Finally, look forward. Time shift into the future; see the big picture. Every assignment you accept should be compared to that larger vision. Analyze where you are going.

How many steps do you still need to take? Is this the road that will get you there? How do you see your purpose playing out on a larger scale? When your vision is clear, it releases you from unwanted burdens and unnecessary distractions that will have no impact on your ultimate goal and purpose in life.

PRIORITY NEEDS A PLAN

Once you gain clarity, you must develop a priority plan. The word priority comes from the word "prior," which means first and most important. Priority demands simplicity. With so many competing demands vying for our time and attention, we must simplify what's essential in our lives.

Doing more doesn't equate to *accomplishing* more. In fact, I have found that having a ton of things to accomplish makes it easier to end up doing nothing. Why? Because a long "to do" list feels overwhelming. If you are a Type A personality like me, your number one goal in that case is to complete *everything* on your list. You embark on an unrealistic mission to get it all done before sundown. Of course, you don't know which task should come first, or what should get more attention, time, and energy. By the time you determine what your priority should be, you have remembered a half dozen *new* items that should be on the list! Sound exhausting? It is. And it leads to frustration, anxiety, and a lack of progress.

In his bestseller, *The One Thing*, Gary Keller reinforces the importance of simplicity, the principle that we accomplish more when we focus on less. He writes, "Going small is ignoring all the things you could do and doing what you should do. The way to get the most out of your work and your life is to go as small as possible. Extraordinary results are directly determined by how narrow you make your focus."[18]

This seems counter-intuitive to many of us. We tend to think (and have often been taught) that big results come from doing more things. But this creates competition between your various tasks and assignments. You have to split your focus and delegate only part of your energy and passion into each assignment. If you have ten projects, you cannot possibly put more than an average of 10% of time and energy into each one. This results in limited success over a longer period of time. However, if you can narrow your focus and concentrate your energy, you can achieve greater results in less time.

Patricia is a high-level executive in the social services arena. She had created an extensive list of personal and professional goals she wanted to accomplish. No matter how often she started on her goals, the results were the same: She achieved nothing. After three years of stopping and starting she became frustrated and overwhelmed. We examined her list together and, of course, discovered that she had far too many "priorities" she was trying to accomplish at one time. I helped her narrow down the list by asking, "Out of everything you *could* do on this list, which one speaks directly to your center?" She immediately identified two items on her list. Her list of "priorities" suddenly sharpened, from twelve things to two. She learned the concept that less really is more.

YOUR PURPOSE IS YOUR PRIORITY

Your priority plan needs to promote your center or core mission. Your center includes your signature passion and purpose (as we discussed in Chapters 1 and 2). It is the driving force of your energy. It creates your success zone. It is impossible to work out of your center when you're focused on multiple things. You are more successful when operating in what you were born to do than when you try to accomplish all you *could* do. To protect your center, you must become vigilant at filtering out the opportunities and requests that distract you from what makes you successful.

Go back to your answers on the Purpose-Finder Questionnaire in Chapter One. Ask of each item on your priorities list above, "Does this line up with my purpose?" For example, my purpose is to empower women and organizations to overcome obstacles and embrace their original intention. Someone recently suggested that I help a church's youth organization. I was tempted, because I love young people and could see myself being successful in that endeavor. But just because I *could* do something, doesn't mean I *should*. It would have taken me away from my passion and purpose, and my current priority of finishing this book and taking my women's ministry to the next level.

Secondly, your priority plan should be developed around your central passion. When you use your passion as the barometer, you will scale down your "to do" list. Remember, passion is the emotional intensity you feel toward your assignments. Take a step back and reflect on all you are doing; list them. Ask of each item, "Does this put me on an emotional high? Does it excite me? How fulfilling is it?" Rate each item by numbering it from 0-10 (10 = you couldn't be more excited about it, 0 = it bores you or you hate it). Then circle the lowest-ranked items on your list and set out to eliminate them or delegate them to someone else.

PRIORITIZE YOUR TIME

Every good priority plan will also need a time management component connected to it. A few years ago I went to see a movie titled *In Time*. It was a futuristic science fiction film in which people were genetically engineered with digital clocks on their forearm. In order for them to live past twenty-five years old, they had to work for and buy time. Time had become a universal currency.

Although we don't have genetic clocks on our arms, time is a commodity for us, too. Who doesn't wish they had more time? I often look at résumés of top leaders and wonder how in the world they had time to accomplish all they did? I tell myself that they must have had nannies and chauffeurs and various other support systems. That may have been true in some cases, but in all likelihood the secret of their success was that they respected the value of time.

You have been given the same amount of time as everyone else on the planet. Your world spins at the exact same rate as everyone else's. No one—no matter how rich, smart, or well-rounded they may be—has more than the same seven days a week, twenty-four hours a day, sixty minutes in an hour than you have.

Time is opportunity—opportunity to complete your goals and move closer to your dreams. But opportunity and opposition often share the same space. There will always be challenges that will limit your ability to use time. I call these challenges "opponents" of time. How you respond to the opponents of time will determine what you are able to produce.

I used to procrastinate, waiting until the last moment to begin a project. Because I didn't use time wisely, taking advantage of the opportunity to prepare, the finished product I offered was good, but not great. I hid behind the excuse that I didn't have enough time. It took me years to realize that I had plenty of time. The real issue was that I didn't manage my opponents of time, which were doubt and fear.

One of the myths I've always believed is that to be successful we must be great time managers. But how do you manage time? We can't control time. Time moves whether we want it to or not. Instead of watching the clock to try and manage time, we can manage our oppositions that come to hinder us from accomplishing our goals. Doubt, fear, competing responsibilities, and too many commitments are the opponents of time that sabotage our ability to focus on what should be a priority in our lives.

PERFECT THE ART OF SAYING "NO"

How often have you found yourself sacrificing your "yes" to accommodate people who can't handle your "no?" Approval-seekers, rescuers, and people-pleasers over-commit themselves for the sake of maintaining connection and acceptance in relationships. Such people believe that if they say "no" they will damage the relationship. The truth is, saying "no" does not damage a relationship; if it looks that way, it's a sign the relationship was already flawed. Saying "no" actually strengthens relationships, as it gives people the opportunity to understand and respect your boundaries.

Most of us have boundaries, but few of us are adept at maintaining them or effectively communicating them to others. Consistently saying "yes" (when you *should* or *want to* say "no") means you have to abandon or shift your boundaries for the benefit of others. When you do that, however, you are letting other people determine how much space you get to occupy.

Saying "no" isn't difficult only for people who fear rejection or abandonment; it's also difficult for the high achiever who finds herself coming up with new ideas every day. She over-commits and overloads her priorities list because she fears that focusing on one isn't enough. She believes that if she doesn't "do more," she will lose an opportunity. But here is a reality check: How much more could you have accomplished in reaching your past goals if you hadn't sacrificed so much time in pursuing new commitments? Not only do we need to practice the art of saying no to others; sometimes we have to say no to ourselves.

Learning to say "no" is a skill you have to practice. It not only takes courage and tenacity, it also takes the desire to move forward in your dream. I decided that if I had to say "no," it was simply because I chose to say "yes" to something more important. A good friend of mine texted me recently: "Saying no is so hard, but saying yes is killing me." When the consequences begin to outweigh the benefits, saying "no" becomes essential to keeping your dream alive.

So when is saying "no" appropriate? For many women, the moment they realize how much time they lost by taking on unnecessary commitments, they want to say "no" to everything and everyone. But this is unrealistic. There are some assignments you can't refuse, especially if they are connected to your employment. But you can begin to negotiate how and when those things get accomplished.

Recently, a good friend was sharing with me her struggles at work. She had a demanding boss who would change the team's priorities every single day. She became overwhelmed and frustrated with trying to understand which direction to pursue. She couldn't tell him "no," as it may have cost her the job. Instead, she decided to tell him what her changing priorities would cost the team and the project. She would say something like, "I can accomplish project A if you like, but it will mean that Project B will no longer be a priority." Her boss didn't like the approach, but her clear communication had its effect.

When you are considered the "go to" person among your friends, family, and place of employment, saying "no" is that much harder. You have taken on the role of carrying everyone else's burdens and problems for so long that it can feel like everything depends on you and saying "no" will seem selfish and heartless. However if saying yes robs you of the ability to be effective in other areas, then saying no is a priority. Helping others build their dreams and reach their goals is noble. However your desire to help others catch up to their dreams, will ultimately put you behind schedule.

I coached one woman who was a social worker and spent almost every day fixing the problems of not only her clients but also her family and friends. She lacked the energy and time to focus on pursuing her own dreams, but didn't know how to stop rescuing others. I knew that it would do little good to tell her to stop helping others. True helpers love to help. So I told her, "You're not going to stop helping others, because helping is your center. From now on, however, you're going to help them in a different way. You're going to help them by helping you first." This one statement freed her to pursue her dreams without the sense of abandoning the ones she loved.

Helping doesn't mean you have to "do" for everyone. Sometimes you can simply point people in the direction they need to go. This also empowers them to grow and stand on their own feet. Other times, you just need to be clear by saying something like, "I love you and would love to help, but my schedule is packed." You don't need to explain all you have to do in order for them to accept your explanation. Be confident in knowing that you have a right to a life that allows you to pursue your God-given destiny and dreams.

Finally, saying no is especially appropriate when a request or an idea runs counter to your top priority. Sometimes saying "no" really means "not yet." Just because you have a great idea or the opportunity seems right, does not mean you should pursue it immediately. Take time to determine if this new assignment falls within your purpose. Go back to your priorities; look at what you have identified as your central focus. What would involvement in this new commitment look like? How much time will this take away from what you are already doing? Will this put you behind schedule? Will this hinder my current momentum?

It may also be good to check your authenticity by asking yourself: Am I willing to invest that amount of time? If not, how much time— if any—am I willing to invest?

If you are contemplating pursuing a new idea, ask yourself, "Is this the right time to try and implement this idea? Can someone else use this idea?" Record the idea in a journal and give yourself a timeframe in which to pursue it. If you are unable to really get the wheels under the idea by the deadline date, it could be God's way of telling you to wait.

When I took the risk and started practicing the word "no," I learned that my fears were exaggerated and usually unfounded. Most of the people who loved and respected my gift eventually gave me the space I needed, even if they were disappointed at first. As a rescuer, I learned that people really don't need as much rescuing as I thought. I didn't need to save them from every crisis. Maturity taught me that a crisis was often an opportunity for them to connect with God in a different way. Finally, saying "no" to the things outside my priorities gave me access to the dream that was inside me.

———— ✺ ————

Time is a womb that gives birth to your next level of greatness. Time provides the incubation period where your idea, dream, or passion can be developed.

Your time is valuable and so is your purpose. When you prioritize your life and focus your vision on what's important, the "greater you" comes forward. You will expand your ability to achieve more freedom, joy, and more of what you were designed and purposed for.

SKILL BUILDER

QUESTIONS FOR REFLECTION

1. Have you ever found yourself overcommitted and over-worked? Write below about one or more of those times.
2. When was the last time you felt the pressure to say "yes" just to please someone?
3. Do you struggle to set boundaries with your time?
4. Do you spend too much time on minor activities?
5. What steps can you to take to free up more time?
6. Go back through the previous chapter and on a separate piece of paper answer the questions listed under Hindsight, Insight, and Foresight.
7. What steps can you take to develop an appropriate priority plan?

Step 6
Activate Your God Intention

CHAPTER 10

Trapped in a Dream

---∞∞∞---

"You don't have to be great to start, but you must start to be great!"

(*ZIG ZIGLAR*).

HAVE YOU EVER HAD "THE running dream?" In the dream, you are running, and no matter how hard you try, it still feels like you are going in slow motion. I have dreamt this numerous times, and the dream always frustrate me because I am either running away from something scary or running toward some urgent deadline. Of course, the dream ends right before I escape, am captured, or reach my destination. I wake up sweating, heart palpitating, but relieved that it was just a dream. I normally lie back down and go back to sleep, but often the same dream resumes.

You may have discovered that trying to move forward in your purpose feels much like that dream. You have the willpower, and are running as fast as you can, but you have no acceleration toward your goals. Worse is the feeling of being trapped in a perpetual cycle of great ideas and good intentions with no results. You have plans—big plans, even—but it seems no matter how many times you tell yourself what you want to do, need to do, or promise to do, your movement seems slow, even non-existent. There is nothing more frustrating than having the will, desire, and even vision to do things, but not having the power to bring it to fruition. There is no worse feeling than having a revelation of what you carry inside yourself and not being able to make it happen.

We often live in two worlds. The "real world," and the world of our dreams. Your dream life is the life you long for, the life you desire to achieve. This is the place we often daydream about and secretly steal away to when our reality is frustrating and disappointing. There is an excitement and euphoric feeling attached to dreaming—so much so, that dreaming can become addictive. Some people get high from being inspired with new ideas, yet fail to truly execute them.

There is nothing wrong with dreaming. Dreams are a blank canvas where God's will is revealed. Dreams are the stage on which your purpose is fulfilled. I believe that God's dreams for your life are always bigger than what you can imagine. When God wants to reveal the magnitude of His plans for us, He often uses the medium of dreams because dreams don't contain boundaries or limits. In other words, you can conceive of anything when you dream.

The problem with dreams, however, is that they show up in a matured state. In a dream, you see only the result, not the process. You see the part where you are successful and possibly becoming rich. This pulls you into the fantasy of dreaming without the reality of understanding the steps or how much work, effort, or resources it will take to fulfill the dream. I have met powerful women who aborted their dreams because they didn't understand the process or because they lacked the necessary resources.

When your dreams outweigh your resources, and you don't have the know-how on bringing those dreams to fruition, you can become content with being inspired, rather than moving to be intentional. You might become satisfied with just dreaming. I call it being trapped in a prison of vision. You can see it, but lack the ability to bring it to pass.

WHY MOST IDEAS NEVER HAPPEN

Steve Jobs taught us that the world doesn't move by money; it moves by ideas. Unfortunately, the graveyard is the richest place in the planet; it is populated by those who died with million-dollar dreams and ideas trapped inside of them. My life coach, Derrick Sweet, once told me that most people die at age twenty-five and get buried at seventy-five. In other words, we often lose the energy, passion, and ambition to follow our hearts, ideas, and dreams early on in life.

There is a television commercial that personifies the beginnings of an idea, by depicting it coming into the world looking like an ugly baby monster. It is hairy, out of place, and not accepted. But with proper nurturing and support it eventually grows into something beautiful. Ideas and dreams often begin inauspiciously. They take time to develop. And their life cycle is short. As a result, most ideas fail to reach maturity.

Once you get over the initial excitement of having an idea, dream, or goal, you face the reality of how to get it started. The voice of your inner critic (we all have one) will begin to argue with your optimism and excitement: *How are you going to get the money? Will people really support you? How do you know it's going to work?* The voice of past failures will quickly try and convince you not to try again. This internal battle can be exhausting. It often leads to discouragement and disillusionment. In the end, we no longer see the idea for what it is—a future blessing. Instead it begins to feel more like another burden to carry.

Finally, ideas represent change. Dreams represent a disruption of the status quo. When we move to fulfill a dream, we are moving to create "a new normal." This is why most people resist change. You may have discovered similar resistance from family, friends, or co-workers to new ideas you proposed. You may have even experienced your own internal resistance to executing a goal. There is a gravitational pull to stay in what is familiar and comfortable. Sometimes it is easier to remain in the safety of what you know instead of venturing into the uncertainty of the unknown.

ENEMIES OF ACTIVATION

So, what's *really* stopping you from getting started? Challenges? Disappointment? Lack of resources? What's keeping you from activating your "God intentions?" Your "God intentions" are not just good ideas, but it's those God-given, soul stirring dreams, and desires that feel imbedded within you.

How many plans have you postponed? How many dreams have you put away, like helium balloons squeezed into a box? Obstacles will always present themselves whenever you desire to do something new. The enemy of great ideas lives in the space between inception and fulfillment.

I am convinced, however, that our greatest enemies are not real and measurable, but rather perceived. The obstacles *seem* real and almost impossible to overcome: Doubt, insecurity, frustration, and procrastination. They create a perception of impossibility and make it difficult for you to see your dreams through to fulfillment. But your perceptions can be challenged and controlled. To activate your God intention you must adjust your perception to match the reality of God's plan for your life. At times, your perceived obstacles are simply opportunities for you to stretch and grow your faith.

There are, however, very real forces beyond our control that can roadblock us from activating our dreams. They may come in the form of life interruptions that are impossible to predict and difficult to manage. Sudden unemployment, loss of a loved one, sickness, or becoming the caretaker of elderly parents are just a few of these roadblocks. Not every interruption is negative; some come in the form of new job opportunities, unexpected promotions, or the arrival of children and grandchildren. These are the more difficult to overcome *because* of the potential emotional and sometimes financial benefits they offer. Either way, these detours threaten to take us away from our intended destination.

Doubt, insecurity, indecision, procrastination, and other life interruptions are enemies of activation. They have their foundation in one word: Fear. It may be fear of moving into something new, of being misunderstood, of disappointing those who depend on us, and fear of the unknown. Fear hides behind excuses, such as, "I don't have time," "I don't know where to start," "No one else has been successful," and—my favorite—"I'm getting ready to do it." Fear can even hide behind our spirituality, and reflect a spiritual lingo that makes it ok to do nothing: "I'm waiting on God," or "I'm praying about it." It is a good thing, of course, to wait on God and pray for guidance. But dependence on God will lead to clarity and resolve, not inertia.

———— ∞ ————

I believe we have given fear more power in our lives than it ought to have. If we allow it, fear can become a self-fulfilling prophecy.

We focus so much emotional energy on avoiding our fears that we actually create the atmosphere for them to come to pass. I believe you can only experience what you believe. In other words, whatever you run away from in life is what you will run into.

In my early years of ministry, I struggled with self-confidence. I didn't believe that speaking was my forte. Before every presentation, I would worry incessantly. I would spend weeks perfecting my notes and practicing every word. But in spite of my preparation, I never did well. My presentations never went as planned; the message didn't really come across to the people the way I had envisioned. Fed up and discouraged, I prayed and asked God to help me fix my presentations. When He answered I sensed him saying, simply, "The problem is *not* in your presentation, but in where you place your energy. You have poured so much energy in not failing that you don't have any energy left to succeed."

What a revelation that was! I had been spending so much energy in dotting every "i" and crossing every "t" that I had nothing left to really touch people, which is where I wanted and needed to succeed. I was so afraid that I wouldn't come across as a good speaker that I didn't take the time to really think through what my listeners needed. I was more focused on getting my presentation "right." I wanted to sound eloquent, to receive approval from my leaders and the people. In the end, what I feared is exactly what I experienced. I failed. I experienced it because I created the atmosphere for it.

The energy you put into avoiding your fears will actually feed them and cause them to grow even bigger. Your need to not fail can become so big that it will shift your focus off what's truly important and slow down (or stall) your progress. In writing this book, for example, I had so much fear about getting every word right that it took months to finish a few chapters. Then one day a good friend of mine, Dr. Harold Arnold, helped me by saying,

"A really good book that is finished is better than a perfect book that remains stuck in your head." What is sabotaging your progress? Are you someone who needs to have all the answers before you move? Do you have to see the whole picture before you take a step? Or maybe you're afraid that you won't measure up to a standard that has been set by other people. Either way, it's time to activate your courage and move beyond the fear.

FEAR OF HEIGHTS

Sometimes it's the fear of *success,* not failure that causes us to put the brakes on our forward movement. I love Marianne Williamson's words: "Our deepest fear is not that we are inadequate. Our deepest fear is that we are powerful beyond measure. It is our light, not our darkness that frightens us."[19]

A few years ago during a summer vacation, my husband and I decided to go zip lining. We had heard how exhilarating and fun this activity was so we decided to try it. In zip lining, you are connected to a little harness hanging from a series of cables stretched between towers or trees. Trainers take you on a dizzying series of flights nine hundred feet in the air from one side of the rainforest to another. Our excursion had about ten stations and each one was higher and longer than the one before. To say I was nervous is an understatement. I was scared.

But flying through the air on a thin line was not the most challenging aspect of this activity. The most challenging aspect was each climb to the next platform. In order to get to the next height or level, we had to carry our equipment and climb. Because we were in the jungles of Mexico, we were climbing incredibly steep mountains. It was laborious, tedious, frustrating, and painful— especially for someone who is out of shape. Many in our group began to cry and complain that they couldn't make it.

It wasn't until I got to the third platform that I realized my fear increased as I climbed higher. Not one to quit or show weakness, I kept climbing. But when I got to the highest level, I became paralyzed with fear. I had never in my life been that high off the ground in an open space. *What if I fall? Are the ropes really that secure? Should they really have ropes this high up here?* It was a strange paradox because I had worked so hard to get there but wanted to go back. I also allowed the negativity of others around me to convince me that being up that high was dangerous and frightening (the truth is, the entire rope course was dangerous from beginning to end!). But the fun decreased and terror increased as my comfort level shrank. I didn't start to question where I was, until I got to a place I had never been.

Most people will never admit they're afraid of succeeding. It doesn't sound right. But have you ever gotten a promotion for which you had worked hard, and after you got it, you thought, "Oh shoot. What do I do now?" It's not that you don't want to succeed; you do. That's why you're reading this book. But going to the next level often puts a demand on an untested and unproven area of your life.

My husband had a dream of becoming a CEO of a health-care agency. He had worked as VP, manager, director, and supervisor, but had never been a CEO. When he got his first position he was ecstatic. But his first few weeks were fear-filled. He wondered, *Will I do a good job? Can I actually do this? Will I measure up to their expectations? Can I sustain progress?* Although these inhibitions didn't prevent my husband from applying for or accepting the position, the fears were real—because getting to a place you have never been will often require you to conquer fears you've never faced.

For some women the fear of success is commonly connected to a fear of being ostracized for obtaining success. I have counseled women who had tons of excuses for why they couldn't go back to college or apply for a promotion they were obviously qualified to receive. When we got to the real issue, several of them admitted that they were afraid of what others would think. Would they still be accepted among family members and friends who were not so successful?

Internally these women told themselves, "I am not worthy!" It's similar to survivor's guilt (the feeling of having done something wrong by surviving a traumatic event when others did not). You feel guilty that your family and friends worked just as hard as you, yet didn't get the promotion or opportunity that you did. Or maybe you stepped into something and don't feel you earned it...so you downplay your accomplishment by saying things like, "Oh, it's nothing," "I don't know how it happened," or "I just got lucky."

The guilt that is associated with going to the next level will rob you of your ambition and sabotage your ability to activate your goals and dreams. It will also encourage you to compromise who and where you are— just to make others feel more comfortable around you.

You were born and destined for more! God has blessed every person on the planet with a gift, talent, or idea to prosper their lives. Regardless of obstacles or life challenges, we all have an opportunity to become more and receive more. Don't allow others to make you feel guilty for utilizing what God has given to you.

ACTIVATE....TO ACCELERATE

While enemies of activation are real, when confronted they can be conquered. We have to work hard to overcome the obstacles of ambition that rob us of the ability to get started and move forward. Silencing the voice of your inner naysayer (and your external critics) takes an everyday commitment. It's also hard work because that inner critic has often disguised itself as the voice of wisdom and reason.

Although I was afraid on that zip line in Mexico, I also wanted to experience flying through the air at a higher altitude. I had to ignore my own internal voice of negativity, and the voices of those around me. When I released the safety and took the leap, I experienced such an acceleration to the other side that it erased all the fear and doubt I experienced during the climb. The moment your desire to succeed becomes greater than your fear, you will create a season of acceleration to everything you have been trying to accomplish.

Let me ask you a question: Do you *really* perceive of your own God given capacity to fly? What if the only thing standing between you and the next level is your *perception* of whether you can make the jump?

If you have gotten this far in reading this book, you probably understand that movement and acceleration doesn't just happen. It is intentional. You have to create the atmosphere for acceleration to occur. Your perception of yourself will dictate the kind of atmosphere you create. You have to believe that you were born fully equipped with the capacity to do great exploits. When you can perceive that there is something greater in you and in your future, it will create an atmosphere of faith and enable you to leap into the life God intended for you.

SKILL BUILDER

QUESTIONS FOR REFLECTION

1. What goals do you want to accomplish by this time next year? List at least three.
2. What most often gets in your way when you try to make progress toward the fulfillment of your dreams?
3. If you knew you couldn't fail, what would your next step be?
4. If you had unlimited resources, how would you approach your goals?
5. What's the most important step you can take toward activating your goals and dreams?
6. What is one obstacle that would transform your life if you overcame it?

CHAPTER 11

Embrace the "F" Word

———— ᵒ𝔤𝔤ᵒ ————

"Don't be afraid of your fears, they are not there to scare
you. They're there to let you know something is worth it"

(C. Joy Bell).

IF YOU *REALLY* WANT TO activate your God intention, don't fight
your fears. It may surprise you to read those words. But stay
with me.

We waste entirely too much time trying *not* to be afraid.
Fear is your body's defense mechanism. It's designed to alert
you to the fact that something is off. Let your fear become your
GPS system to point you to the source of your insecurity and
doubt. Decide if there is any merit to what you feel. Insecurity
or doubt is sometimes a sign that you really are headed in the
wrong direction. If that is the case, there is no shame in seeking out wise counsel. Proverbs 11:14 says, "In the multitude of
counselors there is safety" (NKJV). On the flip side, insecurity
and doubt can be due to a lie that you have always believed. If
that is the case, you must identify the truth and put it in place
where the lies exists.

One of the greatest mistakes you can make in trying to overcome fear is *trying* to overcome it. That sounds nonsensical, I

know. But while we shouldn't let fear stop us, we also shouldn't waste time waiting on fear to go away. As Christians we get stuck in rebuking fear and waiting for fear to leave. Just because you are afraid doesn't mean the journey has to stop. Can you move while you are frightened? The victory is not always a result of you overcoming fear; but in the fact that you kept moving *while* you were still afraid. Sometimes in the midst of overwhelming odds, you just have to "do it afraid."

Fear is a sign that you are pursuing something bigger than your resources—and maybe even yourself. Fear may be your confirmation that you are attempting to activate a God intention. If your God intention doesn't frighten you, it may not challenge you to place your trust in Him. Allow your fears to be the stepping stones to embracing a new level of faith in Him. Use fear to stimulate your faith. Fear can move you into a position of worship and surrender to God. God is not intimidated by what is intimidating you, so let faith in Him crowd out your fear.

FAITH TO FAIL

Fear of failure is commonly behind our inactivity. No one likes to fail, of course; it is a painful experience. From the time we are in grade school to adulthood, our lives are built and conditioned around the idea that we must never fail. In the church, we often receive (and sometimes repeat) the message, spoken or unspoken, that people of faith will not fail. But even a casual look at Scripture teaches us otherwise. Prophets and saints throughout history experienced "failure" of one kind or another, at least from a human perspective. Relationships will let us down, employers will lay us off, and some of the things we try will fail. Why? Because we are human; we are fallible and prone to error—and so is everyone around us. So why do we dread it so much? Why do we live our lives trying to avoid it?

Anything great you intend to do will involve a risk. You and I were not born with a crystal ball to see into the future. This was intentional too. God could have given us a crystal ball, or something similar, but he didn't; instead, He gave us faith.

Paul said, "God has dealt to each one a measure of faith" (Romans 12:3, NKJV). Faith in God gives us the ability to move forward into what we believe exists but can't see. But faith is not static. Faith is movement and participation. Sometimes we wait to move because we want God to give us a better sign. In actuality, we would prefer Him to remove the risk that accompanies our faith. Faith will always involve a risk. Walking by faith is taking a step into the invisible and unknown fully believing that your feet will land on something tangible.

God doesn't always (or often) guarantee the outcome. He promises to stay with you through the journey. In fact, sometimes the growth that occurs in the journey is more important than the outcome. Yes, we all want our efforts to succeed; we want our investments to pay off. But sometimes you receive more by just leaving your comfort zone than in reaching your destination.

You may wonder, *Why waste my time, then, on something that may not work?* Well, what if it did work? Would the next steps be worth the effort? You may ask, *How do I know my effort will be applauded or my plan will be accepted?* Do you know anyone who has died from rejection? Of course not; rejection has never killed anyone, and it won't kill you. You may have actually been through worse than rejection and survived it. You may not have liked it, but you probably grew from it. Further, what if you do fail? What do you believe it will say about you? Failed attempts do not define you. Failure only points to what you attempted. I would rather be known as someone who attempted something great and failed than as a person who just had great ideas but never took big risks.

———— ✤ ————

Instead of fighting your fear, there are two intentional steps of faith you can take to activate your coming season of greatness and embrace "the greater you":

Change your predictability pattern. I love to read. I especially enjoy reading novels. I am less crazy about nonfiction books in general, and self-help books in particular (which is funny, since this book could be classified as "self-help"). A few years ago, I was sharing with a good friend of mine the idea for my business, Purpose by Design, and how I really wanted to expand it beyond its current reach. She suggested that I read a book by Michael Hyatt: *Platforms- Getting Noticed In a Noisy World*. I thanked her but privately dismissed the suggestion. I decided I would just keep doing what I was doing.

When I got home, however, I became aware that my thinking was completely counterproductive to my intentions and my desire to expand my platform. My current skills were limited in the area of social media and marketing, and she had given me a suggestion on how to improve. But because it didn't align with my usual reading habits, I dismissed the idea—a subtle pattern I have followed almost all of my life. Whenever an idea was presented that seemed difficult or required a departure from my usual *modus operandi*, I would dismiss it and look for alternative ways to accomplish my goals. Of course, I never found any alternative ways because while telling myself I wanted change, I didn't want to do what change required.

Have you ever desperately wanted something, yet when the opportunity came for you to receive it, you ran away instead?

Have you found yourself saying what you were going to do, intending to get it done, yet did the exact opposite?

I call it a "pattern of predictability." It's what we do and who we become when we get disappointed, stressed, or afraid. We even revert to it sometimes when we start making progress. Your pattern of predictability always runs counter to your true intentions. You may not be conscious of these patterns because they have long been the norm for you, but they are contributing to your ongoing cycle of habitual behavior and predictable results.

You have probably heard the saying, "If you want what you never had, you have to do what you have never done." You can also say it this way: "If you want to receive the same results, keep applying the same principles." We each have a cycle of thinking and behaving whenever stressors or new opportunities for change are presented in our lives. These cycles or patterns can create roadblocks. These roadblocks can cause an incongruence to occur between what you desire to do versus what you actually accomplish. You may desire to lose weight, but if you are an emotional eater it is a roadblock; your pattern of eating during emotional highs or lows will prevent you from achieving your desire. No matter how often you go to the gym or try to eat right, your cycle will sabotage your progress. If you are not aware of the pattern or cycle, you will become frustrated and see your goal as an impossibility, no matter how achievable it really is.

I used to pray and ask God to give me the chance to stand before large crowds of people and speak to them. Yet each time I was given the opportunity to do it, I would come up with an excuse for why I couldn't. My behavior did not match what I wanted. Why? Because my pattern of predictability got in the way. Challenged to do something that looked overwhelming, I convinced myself that I wasn't good enough. So instead of the opportunity being a blessing and an answer to my heartfelt prayer, I reverted to a cycle of habitual behavior and predictable results.

Desire for more. Sometimes your desire for more will allow you to see your pattern of predictability. But merely desiring more will not change your pattern of what you're already doing. Once you notice the pattern, you must intentionally take steps to do something different.

A good friend of mine was complaining to me about how it seemed that whenever she wanted to set aside time to study in advance for her sermons, her family members would invariably call and ask for help. She would drop what she was doing to rescue them, which usually took up the entire week. She would then have to throw together her sermons in whatever time she had left. She felt as though her best intentions were always thwarted and she was helpless to change things. She believed that the devil was possibly behind this phenomenon. That may be true, but there was another reality operating: Her family always called her for help, and she could not say no. She didn't notice the pattern until she desired more. Her desire for more granted her the opportunity to do something different. She decided to change the pattern.

Mark's Gospel relates an incident in the life of Jesus. Jesus told His disciples to get into a boat and cross over the Sea of Galilee. There was nothing strange about His request. He often asked them to launch out and head to a different place. This particular time, however, Jesus didn't go with them. He sent them. That was when something happened that interrupted their pattern of predictability.

Halfway across the sea, a storm arose and not only hindered their progress, but endangered their lives. No matter how hard they worked at the sails and ropes and oars, their efforts were frustrated. They desperately wanted to move forward, to obtain the safety of the shore, but the wind was against them. They were experienced fisherman. They had dealt with all kinds of weather over the years. But this storm challenged their ability and they struggled for hours, until the fourth watch of the night, right before daybreak, when Jesus came to them, walking on the water. They all thought he was a ghost, but Jesus spoke to them: "Be of good cheer! It is I; do not be afraid."

"Lord," Peter said, "if it is you, command me to come to You on the water." And Jesus told him, "Come" (Matthew 14:27-29, NKJV). Peter then did something that utterly shattered the pattern of predictability—and, with it, the laws of physics! He stepped out of the boat and started walking toward Jesus.

The disciples wanted to get to the other side of the lake. But a storm arose, creating a roadblock between where they were and what they desired. But I believe the storm was strategically allowed, not to derail or delay their hopes, but in order to challenge their pattern of thinking. Their habit as fisherman was to fight to keep the boat upright and afloat in the storm. But Christ came walking on water to show them that there is more than one way to weather a storm and make it to shore. Peter was the only one who had the courage to break the pattern and do something different. He abandoned the boat and attempted something no one had ever done or even attempted. He walked on water.

Peter desired more. He didn't allow his loyalty to the other disciples, to keep him locked in a pattern that was no longer effective. When you are tied to something, you can feel obligated to stay in it. Your obligations to people and places can hinder you from realizing your options. But Peter understood that it's ok to walk away from —what's no longer working.

Sometimes Christ wants to challenge our level of creative thinking whenever a storm or roadblock appears in our path to greatness. Maybe you're reading this and you have a pattern of thinking you've always relied on to get you through certain circumstances. Those patterns may have kept you grounded and worked for you on many occasions. But what happens when a new storm, the likes of which you have never encountered, arises?

How flexible is your faith? How willing are you to change and try something new? Who says you have to follow the same rules for each situation? Is it possible that the same patterns that kept you grounded at one time are now preventing you from flying...or walking on water? Sometimes to walk in a new dimension, you must abandon old strategies that carried you into predictable places.

———

Divine Alignment. You must create alignment between what you desire and what you actually accomplish. To do this you will have to challenge the patterns and systems that you have put in place. We challenge our own systems by taking inventory of what we do, asking, *What gets in my way each time I make progress? What is my cycle? Do I procrastinate, doubt myself? Do I allow others to create roadblocks in my life? How do I respond when I am disappointed? Do I push forward or do I create negative conclusions?*

Next it's important to create agreement and continuity between your thoughts, feelings, and real intentions. To do this you must assess and become aware of what you are feeling, thinking, and believing. For instance, I really wanted to stop hiding and running away whenever I was asked to stand before large crowds. I had to become aware of what my thoughts and feelings were surrounding it. I noticed that I was telling myself,

"The crowd is too big. You don't speak well. What if they don't like you? What if no one is moved?" Those thoughts led to feelings of fear, doubt, and intense insecurity. Ultimately they propelled me into hiding.

What I really wanted was to stand with confidence and allow God to use me to inspire people's faith and hope. How did I build a bridge between my desire and its fulfillment? I had to challenge my pattern of thinking by introducing a new pattern based on the truth. I started to tell myself things like, "If you were not that good, they wouldn't call you," "Yes, the crowd is big but they are human like you," "you don't have the power to move people; God does," and "People may not like you but does that change God's plan to use you?" When I challenged my old strategies, my feelings started to shift from doubt to confidence and courage. I found myself accepting the challenge to stand before large crowds. To this day, I still get nervous, but I have learned to create agreement between my thoughts and feelings and my desired outcome.

———

Your God intentions are waiting to be activated. When you allow the voice of faith to grow louder than your fears, you will find the courage to move into more.

You may have to work consistently to challenge your habitual behaviors. Trace them back to your thoughts and feelings. Always keep your focus on what you really desire to see happen. Keep reaching for that mark. Challenge every internal discrepancy you find. And keep doing it until you discover that what you are feeling and thinking are in agreement with your desired outcome.

Skill Builder

Questions For Reflection

1. Do you find yourself fighting your fears at times?
2. If so, what would it look like to embrace your fears instead?
3. Describe your pattern of predictability. What do you consistently do when you are afraid, stressed, disappointed, or doubtful?
4. What gets in the way when you try to make progress?
5. What is your cycle called? (i.e., procrastination, etc.)
6. Do you allow others to create roadblocks in your life?
7. How do you respond when disappointed?
8. How flexible are you with trying something new?
9. How do you respond to sudden change?
10. What steps can you take to align your intentions with your actions?

CHAPTER 12

Visualize the Impossible

———⁂———

"Why hover in a place called 'Possible' when
God wants us to inhabit the impossible?"

(NIKI BROWN).

CLOSE YOUR EYES FOR TWENTY seconds and let your mind travel
to the place of God's greatest plan and purpose for your
life. Go ahead, I'll wait right here.

Done? Where did your vision take you? How big was your
dream? Wherever that vision ends—is where God's dream for
you begins.

Oprah Winfrey once said on her talk show that what God in-
tends for you goes far beyond anything you can imagine. If you
can see your dream in its entirety, you are probably not dreaming big enough. Our dreams seldom come close to God's real
plans and purpose for us. What we glimpse is a bite-size sample
of the dream. I believe that if He showed us the entire picture,
we may actually faint dead away. Even that bite-size sample may
seem laughable or impossible to you, but it's a picture He wants
you to follow and believe nonetheless.

To activate your intentions you must move from the possible to the impossible. This seems backward because we have

been conditioned to believe just the opposite, which is to take what looks impossible and make it possible. But sometimes our possibilities limit us and keep us from truly stretching our vision and faith. I was speaking to a pastor friend a few years ago and he asked, "So, Niki what's the big picture for you? Where are you in five years?" I opened my mouth to answer and nothing came out. I was stumped. I was even more stupefied because, after counseling and coaching people for years, I couldn't answer that basic question. I eventually offered a generic response, but I could tell that he knew I didn't have a clear picture in my mind.

As I later reflected on that conversation I realized that I had allowed the years of disappointment and lack of opportunities to dim my focus and narrow my options. I didn't have a big picture because I chose to only concentrate on what looked *possible* to me. I was using the past as a reference point for my future goal setting. My prayer requests were consistent with my diminishing expectations.

Seasons of disappointment, closed doors, and failed goals can convince you to lower your expectations and go after *only* those things that seem within your reach. When you narrow your field of vision to just your possibilities, your "big picture" shrinks. While your big picture isn't confined to the size of your circumstances, it *is* limited to the scope of your expectations.

SEEING THE BIG PICTURE

Why is having a big picture necessary to activate God's dreams and intentions for you? Because without a big picture, you become complacent and comfortable. You will settle for life in the comfort zone. But sometimes what you truly desire exists right outside that comfort zone. Dwelling in simple possibilities robs your mind of the creative space it needs to dream. Without a big picture, you will settle for cruise control instead of going into overdrive. The land called "Possible" never really requires any faith. It's only when you start moving toward the realm called "Impossible" that your faith awakens and accelerates.

A few years back I felt led to initiate a women's summit. I had been speaking at women's conferences' and workshops in the surrounding area and had a passion to begin my own. The initial planning and prospect of hosting a summit in my region was very exciting. I had a lot of women who were on board and wanted to help. But when I got to developing the budget and signing the contract my excitement began to wane. I started to wonder, *Who is really going to show up? Did God really tell me to do this? Where am I going to get the money?*

After looking at the numbers and my limited budget, I decided to move forward with the event and prayed for fifty women to be in attendance. Fifty women doesn't seem like much, but to me if seemed like hundreds. After a few weeks, I felt the Lord leading me to increase the contract and move the event to a larger room. I called my good friend Sandy and after discussing it with her, she encouraged me to take the leap. God knows how to connect you with people who can inspire your faith and vision to do more.

Nervously, I called the banquet manager, praying silently that the bigger room was no longer available. But it was available. The banquet manager informed me that I needed to guarantee one hundred and twenty-five women to secure the contract. With trembling knees and shaky hands, I signed the contract for the new room. I was nervous, and very afraid. But as I walked away, I sensed the Lord saying, "I will exceed your expectations!"

I laughed internally and silently thought, *This seems impossible!*

Faith works best in impossible situations. You can't allow your limited resources—and overwhelming odds —to negotiate with faith. You must activate your faith by putting something impossible in front of it. Give your faith a job to do. Create a big picture in your mind that seems almost laughable and present it to God. There is something powerful about believing and reaching for things that are beyond your education, resources, and comprehension. Big pictures will be the catalysts that stimulate consistent growth and movement in your life.

For weeks, I watched in agony as the registration numbers trickled in slowly. I vacillated between faith and doubt. Courage and despair. If I can be transparent, I cried often and wondered, *God, did I really hear you?*

Finally God asked me this question, "Do you have the faith for more?"

This question challenged my faith and eventually led me to understand that while I *desired* more, my faith was not in position to *receive* more.

Quite honestly I wanted my ministry to grow, but I wanted it to happen miraculously on its own. I didn't understand that to receive more required me to operate in a new dimension of faith. Meaning, I had to participate if I wanted to see the impossible come to pass. Every miracle that Jesus performed required the individual's participation. They had to do something to receive the healing, blessing, or miracle that was destined for them.

Your faith has to grow to a place where it can accommodate your future. We serve a big God. Everything He does is big. Your faith must stretch itself to receive His God-sized assignment and blessings. Most of all, you must do something as an act of faith to prepare your season for "the more" that is coming.

On the week of the summit, my registration numbers were still low. I felt myself fighting back a sense of defeat. But the day before I turned in my final count to the banquet manager, I opened my email and there was a flood of new registrations. So many, that my staff and I were overwhelmed. Not only did we meet the expected number, we exceeded that amount and filled the room to its capacity!

How do you envision your future? Is it big enough to scare you? Is it so big that it makes you laugh and shake your head? If so, then you may be looking at the impossible. It only takes one bold move to activate your faith and shift your dreams from ordinary to exceptional.

STUDY YOURSELF HOT

I once counseled a woman who wanted to enroll in college. Her children were older and she thought the time had finally arrived to pursue a degree. However, she kept vacillating and procrastinating. When I challenged her about her behavior, she offered multiple "explanations": The tuition may be too high. She wouldn't be able to carve out the necessary time to study. She heard that her field was saturated and she may not get a job after graduating.

"How much research have you really done on this?" I asked. Her reply: "None."

A major obstacle to activating our dreams and ideas is that we simply don't know enough about where we are trying to go. When I was training to be a minister, my former pastor would tell us that we had to "study ourselves hot." That is, we had to become so immersed in our topic as to create a climate of confidence, enabling us to move forward. In order to make progress toward your goals, you must know what you are getting yourself into. When you don't know enough about your field, you will make assumptions or listen to bad advice which can feed your fear and apprehension about taking the next steps.

So here are some ways to "study yourself hot":

Connect With Your Vision. One way to visualize the impossible and gain confidence is to create vision boards. My good friend, Shawn McLeod, has detailed how vision boards can help you to clarify your vision and dreams while also stimulating your faith and stoking your excitement. In *The Cheat Sheet for Creating Vision Boards That Lead to Discovering Your Purpose*, she writes that "using vision boards can transform the lofty reaching goals and purpose into tangible goals with specific realistic tasks and timelines."[20]

A vision board is literally any type of board on which you display images that represent whatever you want to be, do, or have in life. I have always enjoyed developing vision boards. They not only bring a sense of clarity and focus to dreams, but also show the relationships between different dreams or parts of dreams. Sometimes our efforts are unfocused and ineffective because we can't quite see how certain parts of our dreams are related to each other. Your dreams and ideas are often more connected that you imagined. Vision boards help you connect those dots. They also give you permission to embrace what seems impossible, articulating a story that was previously locked inside your imagination, and thus bringing your most incredible dreams to life.

Become a student of—even an expert in—your field. Knowledge is power. Information breeds security. So research and learn everything you can about your dream or idea. Find out all of the requirements for beginning your pursuit. Do your homework on how much this idea or goal will cost. Will you need to quit your job? If so, how much will you need to sustain you? Put numbers on paper. Compile a spreadsheet (if you don't know how to create a spreadsheet yet, add that to your list!). You may actually find out that it won't cost as much or take as long as you first thought. On the other hand, you might learn that there are a few more steps to take before getting started. Either way, it's better to make an informed decision rather than assumptions about whether or not this is right for you.

After you learn the requirements, move on to become an expert. Find out the industry trends. Study what skill sets and resources are needed. Discover the history of your field and where it may be going in the future. Learn what resources your state and community have to offer. Define what success looks like in this field. How is success measured? Who would benefit the most from your idea? Is the market ready for your idea? Don't be afraid to go the extra mile by taking a webinar, on-line course, or buying a few books on the subject. If this truly reflects your passion, many of these things will be an adventure and joy for you.

Shore up your weaknesses. Confucius once said, "True wisdom is knowing what you don't know."[21] Once you do your homework on your idea, assess your skill sets and strengths. For example, I hate math. No matter how much tutoring I received in school (and my dad was a math teacher!), math remained a weak area for me. For a long time I used it as an excuse for not stepping up as a leader and managing a business or company. But as Marcus Buckingham wrote in *Now Discover Your Strengths*, "...you will excel only by maximizing your strengths, never by fixing your weaknesses."[22]

Just because I was weak in math didn't mean I couldn't be successful. Instead, I had to learn how to manage this weakness in order to be a good leader. So I recruited my husband to teach me the basics of spreadsheets and budgets, and delegated or contracted everything else.

You don't need "all your ducks in a row" in order to move forward. Simply find out what you're missing and shore up your weaknesses. If you are not good at organization, acknowledge it—and then find ways to manage it. Ask others for advice, enlist or employ others who *are* good at organizing things, improve what you can and delegate or contract the rest. Don't allow your weaknesses to slow your progress.

A BRIDGE TO IMPOSSIBLE

You must become intentional about growing and nurturing those ideas and dreams which seem impossible to achieve. The best way to do that is to find a way to connect with the skills and passion of others. It's fair to say that Apple revolutionized the computer industry. If you know the story of Apple's beginnings, you know that it didn't start from a huge financial investment; it started in a garage, with an idea. It began in the mind of a man who had been adopted as a child and dropped out of college. Steve Jobs never finished college, but he had an idea to market and sell computers in a way that gave access to users everywhere. He had a vision, but lacked some skills. Fortunately, he knew someone who had just the skills he lacked: Steve Wozniak. Apple Computers was born.

I have met many well-intentioned leaders and budding entrepreneurs who had phenomenal ideas, but didn't know how to collaborate. They isolated their ideas for fear of competition.

Some did not want to share the credit. Charles Lee, author of *Good Idea. Now What: How to Move Ideas to Execution*, says, "Whenever you come up with a new idea, there is a high probability that it stands on the shoulders of previous thoughts that carried various aspects of your ideas."[23]

Don't build your ideas in a silo. Your revelation needs relationship. In other words, the ideas and dreams inside you need a sponsor, mentor, or coach to help push them farther down the path. Strategic partnerships can create a bridge for you to connect those impossible dreams to stronger resources and a higher level of creativity. They may also help you gain access to a platform or enlarge your audience, thereby increasing your services or revenue.

Your idea may also become a bridge for someone else's dream to be fulfilled. Facebook, Twitter, and YouTube are examples of ideas that transformed themselves into platforms. Numerous businesses have been born, and people discovered, as a result of these platforms that bridged people's needs and passions.

Take a step back and evaluate how your idea or dream may connect with what others are already doing. Find out how your idea fits within the larger world and be ready to collaborate with others in order to expand your influence and exposure.

READY... FIRE...AIM!

In their international bestseller, *In Search of Excellence*, Tom Peters and Bob Waterman came up with the slogan "ready, fire, aim" (instead of "ready, aim, fire") as an execution strategy for businesses. It has become a common phrase in the business world as way of overcoming inertia and pushing them into action. Sometimes businesses tend to get stuck in pre-planning and analyzing every detail in order to minimize risks. Instead the focus should be on taking a step; if it's the wrong step, it's probably still better than inaction, especially if you learn from it and implement corrections to it.

I like "ready, fire, aim," because it's action-oriented. Our need for certainty often causes us to get bogged down in planning and thinking and never get to the point of action. This leads to what some have called "analysis paralysis," where we get ready, then aim…aim…aim…aim… aim! Many good ideas never get off the ground because the research or preparation phase is never finished.

However, "ready, fire, aim," does not eliminate the need for wisdom. Wisdom is needed for every step in the process of bringing a dream to fruition. Proverbs 4:7 says, "Getting wisdom is the wisest thing you can do! And whatever else you do, develop good judgment" (NLT). A divine balance of faith, wisdom, and action results in success. You will never have all the answers. You will never know with 100% certainty that you're taking the right step. But it's foolish to think there is no time to think. Don't move blindly; exercise faith. Faith does enable you to wisely plan out your steps. But "faith without works is dead" (James 2:20, KJV). Don't stay content in planning; you must take action too.

Sometimes the only thing standing between you and your next level is not an open or closed door; it's your decision to turn the doorknob—or even to lower your shoulder and break through the barrier. Your perception and initiative to walk by faith, will make a greater difference than more analysis and planning.

You may be telling yourself that you are waiting on God, but often God is waiting on you to agree with what He has put inside you. *He* is waiting on *you*...the "greater you" to take a step. Will you be nervous? You should be. You should probably be afraid. If you are not, it could be a sign that you are relying on your own strength and maybe your vision isn't big enough yet. But if what you see ahead makes you nervous and at times fearful, it's your time to *activate*.

Skill Builder

1. What's your Big Picture?
2. Describe where you will be in five years.
3. What are your "impossible" dreams?
4. Where do you need to take immediate action on those dreams?
5. Where do you need more planning and preparation?
6. What further steps can you take to connect your dreams and ideas with others who have similar passions and complementary skills?

Step 7
Trust the Transition

CHAPTER 13

Time to Shift

——∞——

"Perhaps the butterfly is proof that you can go through a great deal of darkness and become something beautiful"

(UNKNOWN).

MOST KIDS CAN'T WAIT FOR the last day of each school year. Not me.

I never liked the last day of school as an elementary student. I was always a nervous wreck. I could never really enjoy all the end-of-the-year festivities because I dreaded the final report card which was given at the end of the day.

I wasn't worried about my grades, though. I was completely consumed about which new classroom I would be assigned to for the following year. *Will I have any friends? Will I like the new teacher? Will the teacher like me?* My agony extended through the summer. Looking back, I realize now: I simply hated change.

Change is inevitable. We know that, of course. But no matter what age, stage, gender, or culture we are, most of us have a tendency to resist change. We resist change in our jobs, ministries, routines, careers, relationships, and even in our physical bodies. Why? Because there is security in familiarity and predictability. We feel more comfortable where we are than in the "unknown" and the unpredictable. Structure and predict-ability help to sustain the illusion (and it *is* an illusion) that we are still in control of our world. Change, however, makes us feel vulnerable. It forces us to question and wonder. In our fast-paced society, who really wants to take the time to learn a new process? Why would you want to embrace a new set of rules, relationships, or requirements? What was wrong with the old ones?

Transition is defined as the "status of changing from one state to another." Transition is movement from where you used to be to where you are going. Whether it is voluntary or invol-untary, transition is by nature disruptive. It is often unsettling. It creates a sudden break in your norm. Often you have no point of reference to help you gain clarity on where you are going or what is up ahead. Life-as-you-know-it is changing into Life-as-you-don't-know-it.

In a time of transition, you discover that the principles and rules that guided in you one season are now being challenged in this new season. Transition will redefine your perspective. It will challenge your faith, your way of thinking and behaving, your relationships. Feelings of fear, confusion, stress, anxiety are to be expected, so it's easy to understand why our first in-clination is resistance.

As I am writing this book, I have just relocated to a new city after living somewhere else for almost forty years. I am a home-body, and this is the first time I have lived far away from family and friends (even during my college years I opted to stay at home and commute back and forth; I moved out of my parents' home to get married and have since lived, worked, and minis-tered in familiar surroundings all of my life). But one phone call and a job-offer-you-can't-refuse changed everything. Now, nothing is familiar. Our house and neighborhood are new to us. The school system works differently. Accents sound strange.

The people and community are not what I am accustomed to. Everything is different.

In my first few months, I rejected where I was because it didn't look like where I had been. Eventually, I found excitement in the possibility of starting over and being released from the expectations of other people. Sometimes you can be moving at such a high rate of speed for so long that you lose a sense of yourself. This transition was my opportunity to let go of what's familiar, and to redefine myself. Change is an interruption, but it can be a good one. It can stop the merry-go-round of life. It can allow you to take a step back, breathe, and hit Reset.

FINDING THE SIGNS

Most transitions don't happen suddenly. It's a gradual shift that occurs first in your heart and spirit before it manifests itself outwardly. It is felt but unseen. In *Who Moved My Ladder?* author Sam Chand describes the internal shift this way:

"For fourteen years, I had dreamed and worked hard as I ascended that golden ladder. I loved the people, the work, the challenges, and the excitement of going up each rung. One day, however, something changed. (I write "one day" but something had been going on for months until the day I became aware.) "Who moved my ladder? This isn't where I want to stay, I said."[24]

Does this sound familiar? Have you ever gotten to a place where *who you were* no longer connected with *where you were*? Transitions are often most difficult in the beginning, when it's hard to identify and diagnose what is causing the silent unrest we feel. There are people who have been stuck in transition for years because they didn't know how to diagnose what they were sensing. They show up physically, but their heart and mind is someplace else.

There are several common signs that you are in transition:

A sense of unfulfillment you can't explain. As Sam Chand explains in his book, transition is happening when you get to the top of the ladder (or maybe even the middle) and things you once found pleasurable and rewarding no longer satisfy you.[25] You may think there is something wrong with the people, or the present assignment. You may wonder who moved your ladder. But no one moved it; *you* moved, and the ladder didn't come with you. When your purpose and your position are no longer in alignment, you will experience a sense of unfulfillment, one that is not easily attributed to any external circumstances.

A feeling of restlessness followed by forced busyness with no results. I was in transition for at least three years before I became aware of it. I was restless, and attributed it to the ministries I oversaw needing more activities. So I recruited more volunteers and created more programs, all in the hope of quieting the growing storm within me. However, though I was busier than ever, I assessed my efforts and realized I hadn't produced any measurable results. There was no evidence of new growth, particularly compared to the amount of energy I had invested. But I kept repeating the same cycle of frustration and confusion: The harder I worked, the less I produced, and the more restless I became.

Increased frustration with what's familiar. A Dunkin Donuts commercial in the 1980s depicted, "Fred the Baker" trudging out of bed and off to work, half asleep, muttering the now-famous line, "Time to make the donuts." It was an award-winning commercial and may have sold a lot of donuts, but it probably dissuaded some people from applying to work at Dunkin Donuts. Who wants to get up that early, like Fred? Especially when it looked like drudgery to many viewers.

When you are in transition, the tasks, projects, and assignments that used to challenge your skills and abilities are no longer a challenge. You feel as if you can do your job with one eye closed. Not only that, perhaps, but you can do your job, your neighbor's job, and possibly your supervisor's job, too. This is a sign that you have outgrown the parameters of where you are. "Familiar" becomes boring. Friendships, hangouts, and hobbies have ceased to be exciting or stimulating. I call this being trapped in the cycle of the mundane. You are doing the same thing every day out of habit, expectation, and obligation.

Unwillingness to accept what's been expected. The moment you embrace who you are and what you have to offer the world, it's hard to go back to who "*they*" want you to be. The expectations of others no longer fit your vision of who you desire to be or where you are attempting to go. You grow increasingly more agitated at the requests and demands that are placed on you. You no longer want to fit within the prescribed mold that friends, family and possibly you have built. The demands and expectations may be the same as they were, but *you* have changed.

A desire for more, with no clarity on how to move. The most frustrating aspect of transition is that you want more, but you may not know what "more" looks like or even how to go about getting it. You pray and it seems that God remains silent. You may even try to explain yourself to people around you, but they don't understand, and you don't know how to express what you're feeling. You may even have been accused of not appreciating your blessings. But deep down you know that you are not ungrateful; you're just not satisfied, because you're in transition.

Emotional and Physiological Signs. Transition and change can also wreak havoc on our emotions. Some of the symptoms include feelings of sadness, irritability, melancholy, lack of energy, irritability, crying, guilt, fear, stress, and anxiety. If this time of transition lasts too long, it can lead to depression and psychosomatic issues such as stomach pain, headaches, weight loss, and weight gain.

MANAGE THE SHIFT

While transitions may cause you to feel as if your life is suspended in mid-air, it's actually moving you. You can't always see the movement, but you are growing, if slowly, and moving toward new and unchartered territory. Your ability to navigate transition will be determined by your ability to do the following:

Embrace what is. You will never make significant movement forward until you acknowledge where you are. As painful as it may be, you must accept the reality that the door to your current season is closing. When I finally understood what was happening in my time of transition I felt a mixture of relief and sadness. I didn't want the previous season to end. I still had ideas and dreams I wanted to execute. I had built relationships that were important and significant to me. But if I wanted to experience what God had in store for me, I had to accept "what is." If I wanted to finally step into more, I had to embrace the fact that God's design for me was not to stay where I was forever. I had to let go of "now" in order to move on to what was "next."

Remember, some seasons in your life are designed only to help you build a platform for where you are going. Those seasons allow you to grow and mature. They help to define and sharpen your vision. They become the catalyst for a new level of relationship with God. But once you reach the point of maturity, change and transition is inevitable. A pastor friend of mine, Karen Orlando, told me that some plants were meant to live in greenhouses, while others will die if they stay in the greenhouse too long. The greenhouse while safe, can also smother a plants ability to rise to its full potential.

You carry something that is greater than your environment. You may not have a clear idea of what it is, but you *sense* that your potential exceeds your current status.

You can choose to fight change or embrace it. If you fight it, you will probably create a permanent season out of one that was supposed to be only temporary. You will also smother gifts and talents you could have developed, if you had not been locked in a place that stifled your growth.

When you embrace change, however, you invite God to create the space you need to spread out and grow what has been developing in you for years. And embracing change saves you unnecessary struggle and conflict, too; it helps you to discover the peace you need to begin moving on.

Release what was. Letting go is hard to do. Though I embraced the fact that I was moving, it remained very hard to let go of everything I had been working at for years. I trained other people to take my place and started letting go of some of my regular duties, of course, but I still found myself trying to lead and direct. I came to realize that I had allowed those assignments to define me. I really didn't have a vision of who I was apart from the ministry I had led. As long as I was working in the ministry, I had a clear sense of my identity; I felt secure and comfortable. But apart from it, I felt lost. Have you ever been attached to a place, person, or something else for so long that you no longer see yourself? That's where I was.

Sometimes letting go is difficult because of *how* the transition took place. The death of a loved one, separation, divorce, an unexpected breakup or job loss, and abandonment are changes that can make it difficult to find closure. When we lack closure, we will try and make sense of the loss ourselves. This can keep us hanging onto things in our past and prevent us from shifting into our future.

A successful transition will disengage you from the things and relationships that are not meant to follow you in the shift. It also expands your vision, giving you a broader perspective, a larger worldview. When you release what was, you will discover that there *is* more. I learned that the world was a good deal larger than my little town and beloved church. There was a much bigger world waiting for me.

I think this is one of the most crucial and difficult steps in our journey towards full transition. In order to let go of the past and release what was you will need to:

Let go of the guilt. Guilt is often the silent culprit that keeps us tied to things that no longer define us. We feel guilty walking away from people who depended on us (whether they should have or not). We worry that maybe we are abandoning them and it's a sign that we no longer love them. I have heard many people say, "Well, I can't just leave my job, can I? Who will take on my responsibilities? How will this affect everyone?" Those who have lost a loved one or been through divorce often feel guilty at the prospect of finding love and happiness once again.

Guilt is built on perception. For example, you may carry a belief that not "being there" for others is a failure on your part, that it's not right to live your own life and pursue your own goals. Sometimes the people in your life can influence such beliefs by discouraging you from letting go. You may hear things like, "Are you sure this is the right time?" "Why would you want to do that, when you are so good at this?" and "I still need your help, what am I going to do?" You may also experience the silent treatment, anger, and resentment from those around you.

When you are preparing to shift into a new season, the parameter for your relationships will change. Some of your close connections will be unable to understand your transition. The same people who may have supported you in the past, may not have the capacity to support you in this new endeavor. But don't fight the shift. It's ok to renegotiate your current relationships. Ask God to give you the grace to say goodbye.

The guilt that is associated with letting go will convince you that you're being selfish. It will hijack your efforts and prevent you from reaching your goals. Guilt will sap your energy and sabotage your success. It will undermine your future fulfillment.

To break free from guilt you must comfort yourself with the knowledge that those you love will survive without you. Why? Because, while you can be responsible *to* other adults, you are not responsible *for* them; God is responsible for them. He loves them more than you do. He will make sure His plan and purpose is fulfilled in their lives. Sometimes letting go of loved ones can actually help them to connect with God *better* than holding onto them would.

Secondly, you have to believe that you *deserve* to move on. You deserve more. Your life doesn't end with the person who left you or the season that's ended. Just because you experienced a loss doesn't mean you have to *become* lost with it. Remind yourself of God's call and commission. Everything God created has an internal mandate to grow and change. You are no different. Isaiah 43:19 says, "Behold, I will do a new thing, Now it shall spring forth; Shall you not know it?" (NKJV). For every loss, there is the opportunity to gain something new.

Cry your way through it. This may sound unhealthy, but I cried for weeks leading up to my departure from New Jersey. In spite of that, I had a conviction that even though I didn't want to go, I couldn't stay. I knew we were making the right choice, but I still cried many tears. Tears are a way of cleansing your soul. God never tells us not to cry. In fact, our tears are so valuable to God that the psalmist sang, "Put my tears into Your bottle" (Psalm 56:8, NKJV). God is comfortable with our tears. It is healthy to grieve what you are leaving behind. Give yourself space and time to do that. Write your feelings in a journal. Share your thoughts with loved ones who have been supportive of your transition. However, don't allow your tears to suggest that what you are leaving behind is better than what is ahead.

Celebrate what will be. The space between what used to be and what will be is understandably filled with uncertainty, doubt, and fear. The most difficult part of moving from New Jersey to Kentucky was that I knew exactly what I was leaving behind, but had no clue what opportunities and blessings awaited me ahead. For months after arriving in Kentucky, I felt hopeless and discouraged because I didn't know my next steps. Transition requires you to exercise faith and trust in God while you are waiting in the hallway between yesterday and tomorrow. I quickly learned that I was in a holding pattern and God was testing my faith. Could I believe that the God who was present and faithful in my past was with me now?

The simple truth is that a change in your life does not constitute a change in God's divine plan. He is "the same yesterday, today, and forever" (Hebrews 13:8, NKJV). God's plan for you is not threatened by the changes you experience. Satan's plan, however, is to rob you of the joy and excitement that comes with entering a new season. You could be so worried and confused about what you left behind that you miss the opportunity to enjoy and prepare for what's coming next. But when you exercise faith in the transition, your vision will mature and help you to see beyond your present circumstance and limited understanding. You will discover that in the uncertainty is a certainty that God's purpose is being divinely fulfilled in you.

Find ways to celebrate what is coming. Rejoice in the fact that God is making all things new. The same things that create feelings of confusion and fear can also stir up excitement, anticipation, and peace.

Choose to believe that you are stepping into more and not less. Take out time to enjoy the journey rather than bemoaning the process. Don't allow what you left behind to hinder you from embracing what could be your best season yet.

SKILL BUILDER

1. Read back over the signs of transition listed in this chapter. Can you identify with any of them? If so, which ones?
2. Do you feel bored and unchallenged with your current assignment?
3. If you are in transition, what are some steps you can take to embrace transition instead of resisting it?
4. How have you struggled to let go of what was?
5. Take out a scrap piece of paper. List what you are leaving behind. Include both positive and negative things. On the other side, list what you will be gaining *and* what you hope to gain.
6. What steps can you take to begin celebrating what will be?

CHAPTER 14

Re-Evaluate Your Worth

—⚬⚬⚬—

"Always know the difference between what you
are getting and what you deserve"

(UNKNOWN).

TIMES OF TRANSITION ARE EXCITING times to reset yourself, embrace new opportunities, and expand your capacity. Even if your transition is the result of a divorce, loss of a loved one, job change, relocation, or an empty nest, you may discover that you now have a lot time and quiet space. Many people struggle with empty space and immediately seek out new relationships and things to do. But this space and time can also be a strategic opportunity for you to reevaluate your skills, abilities, and gifts. Transition affords you the ability to prepare yourself for what's coming next, whether it is a new job, relationship, or the opportunity to travel or start a business.

Once I overcame my initial melancholy about moving, I finally took notice of the quiet. I didn't have the stress, phone calls, emails, or demands on my time that had previously plagued me daily. It was a perfect time for me to dust off my journal and review the goals and dreams I had pushed to the side. I realized that finishing my book was my first passion and priority. I had been working on it little by little for over two years, but could never get any momentum going because of all the other hats I was wearing. I decided that this was a God-ordained season for me to not only finish my book, but to bring other incomplete projects to completion.

What about you? How many projects and ideas do you have floating around in your head or written down on scrap paper that you want to work on? Have you ever told yourself (or God) that if you only had the time...? Well, maybe now you do. Resist the temptation to reproduce your past life by doing exactly what you used to do. Take time to re-evaluate your goals, dreams, ideas, and passions. Transition is often the optimal time to get yourself ready for what the new season holds for you.

PROFIT FROM THE SHIFT

Now is the perfect time to take advantage of the space that exists between the "now and the not yet." In my workshops I encourage my participants to: "profit from the shift." Meaning, now is the opportune season to utilize whatever new schedule or down time you may have. Now is a great moment to be intentional and reposition yourself for next level success. Don't waste a lot of energy on what happened in your last season. Look forward and begin to plan.

While you are waiting for what's next to come, here are several ways that you can profit from the shift:

* Determine your priorities and develop a priority plan (review Chapter 11)
* Evaluate your skills, abilities, strengths, and current resources (i.e., income, support etc.).

- Strengthen what's missing by reading books, taking a class, enroll in school or course, join a support group, or go to coaching/counseling.
- Get connected to your new surroundings by meeting your neighbors, coworkers, joining your local business and professional organizations and churches.
- Prepare your mind by envisioning what it will mean to achieve new success.

KNOW YOUR WORTH

Transition offers you an opportunity to reassess your value. One of the first commitments I made in my season of transition was to not allow any new assignment to undervalue my worth. As much as I loved empowering and helping people, I often gave away my services for free. I have undergraduate and graduate degrees in my profession. I invested money in certification programs and training courses. I have years of professional experience in my field. Yet I often accepted jobs and roles that paid me a fraction of what my time, effort, skills sets were worth. I sat around hoping others would notice the disparity between my worth and my wages. But, of course, when you don't know your true value, you give others permission to assign you one. Few people will argue your price when it's "free." Looking back, I had no one to blame but myself. I wanted to be accepted. I wasn't fully convinced myself of the value I had to offer, so I never assigned the proper value to my gifts, time, and efforts.

Don't make that mistake. Assess the value of what you have to offer the world. What is your time, energy, resources, knowledge, experience, gifts, and talents worth? What is the "greater *you*" worth?

You may be coming out of a damaging relationship where you gave way more than you should. Take time to evaluate what made you think it was okay to do that. How should things be different now? What should be better the next time? What steps are you willing to take to honor and protect what you carry inside yourself?

If you have spent years downplaying and undervaluing what you have to offer, you may find it difficult to re-assess your worth. If that is the case, go and ask the people who love you. You probably have friends and family who have been urging you to see yourself differently and value yourself and your time more highly. You may have brushed aside their comments, but it may be time now to listen and heed what they've been saying.

I want to be clear: There is nothing wrong with offering your gifts for little or no pay. God gave you your gifts and talents to serve others. And the truth is you can probably never be adequately remunerated for what it cost to be who you are, get where you are, and do what you do. However, there *is* something wrong when we cooperate with others in devaluing what God has given you and done with you. You're past experiences, gifts, and talents were given not only to bless others, but also to prosper you. Remember the parable of the talents? Those resources were given to those servants to use however they chose, but they were commended when they produced a return on the investment. And the bigger the return, the more they were commended.

God desires for us not only to be blessed. but to be abundantly blessed. We were created to prosper. Deuteronomy 8:18 says, "Remember the Lord your God, for it is He who gives you power to get wealth" (NKJV). And the Apostle John wrote, "Beloved, I pray that you may prosper in all things and be in health, just as your soul prospers" (3 John 1:2, NKJV). Embracing your greatness, the "greater you" will require you to own the value of your gift and what you have to offer the world. If you don't know the value of it, no one else will either.

It's easy to forget that life itself is a constant transition. Even if you stay in one job, maintain the same relationships, and live in one house all your life, you will still experience transitions. A life of intentional greatness means trusting God through the transition and cooperating with His intended outcome, with full assurance that while we go through life changes we are connected to the One who never changes.

Skill Builder

Questions For Reflection

1. How can you shore up your weaknesses?
2. Where do you need to grow?
3. List the background, skills, education, and resources you possess that add to your value.
4. How will things be different in this new season of your life?
5. What do you want to see happen in this new place in your life?
6. What are your time, energy, and resources worth?
7. What steps are you willing to take to truly honor your gifts and talents?

Step 8
Harvest Your Moment

CHAPTER 15

More in the Moment

⸻⸻ ❦ ⸻⸻

*"While you may be waiting for a "moment" of greatness
to come, God is expecting you to create that moment"*

(NIKI BROWN).

GREATNESS DOESN'T JUST HAPPEN. You create it. Moment by moment. With each deliberate step, you create forward progression. Perhaps you have heard someone say, "It's not the destination that's important but the journey." It's true. The journey is what matters. Sometimes we get so anxious to get to tomorrow that we forget to nurture the moments of today that will carry us there. Every moment is a seed. It is small. It looks and feels insignificant. But it carries within itself a harvest. Its destiny is to produce more.

The harvest doesn't occur on its own, however. The harvest requires a convergence of soil, sunlight, irrigation, and time, all happening simultaneously and moment-by-moment. It will often seem that your life is surrounded with similar paradoxical moments of hope, discomfort, struggle, and time (which may often seem to be standing still). But the result is something that vastly outgrows and becomes greater than its humble beginnings.

How you respond to each moment will determine how you enter the next one. I often hear people say, "I'm just waiting for my season." But *every* season is your season. Embracing "the greater you" means owning every moment as an opportune season, a divine space in time to do something that will lead to your next harvest. Every season—whether it is filled with excitement, confusion, or difficulty—is an opportunity to live out aspects of God's ordained plan for you to achieve more.

The question is, what type of season are you in? Is this a season of sowing? Growing? Or reaping? When you correctly identify it, you can respond to this particular season with faith rather than frustration. Frustration is often a result of placing the right expectations on the wrong season. You may be in a time of planting, but if you are expecting a harvest in this season you will be disappointed. Or maybe this is a time for reaping in your life, but you are still planting instead of enjoying the fruits of your labor. But when you know what moment you are in, faith in God will enable you to respond appropriately. This faith is more than just knowing He is real. It's a deep faith and trust that whatever is happening, God is working out every detail and every moment for our ultimate good.

You Had It All Along

As wonderful as this may sound, it is even greater to know that you *belong* in the moment. It is a tragedy to miss your moment because you didn't think you had what *it* takes to enter the moment. Only to realize you were carrying *it* all along. We often run from troubling and stressful events in our lives, but the gifts and abilities you were given were designed not only to prosper you, but also to sustain you through every challenge.

The Bible tells a story that I think speaks to this. The widow of a prophet was in serious debt. Her husband's death left her destitute and with no means to pay her debts. In that day and age, a creditor could enslave debtors or members of their family as a way of settling a debt. So this widow, who had two sons, ran to the prophet Elisha.

"Your servant my husband is dead," she said, "and you know that your servant feared the Lord. And the creditor is coming to take my two sons to be his slaves."

You might expect Elisha to ask her what she owes. You might expect him to offer to talk to the creditor or raise a collection from the other prophets to help her pay her bills. But Elisha did none of those things. He wanted her to see something more.

"Tell me," he said, "what do you have in the house?"

She said, "Nothing…but a jar of oil."

In those days, oil was a valuable commodity. It was often used to anoint prophets, priests, and kings. But she answered, "Nothing…but a jar of oil." She had the anointing substance of kings, priests, and prophets but said the oil was nothing. She couldn't see the value of what she possessed because of where she was.

Elisha told her to obtain as many pots, pans, and other containers as possible, and pour the oil into those vessels. The widow was obedient and borrowed as many vessels as she could. She and her sons poured out that limited quantity of oil. They poured and kept pouring until it filled every available jar.

She told Elisha what had happened. He registered no surprise. He simply told her, "Go, sell the oil and pay your debt; and you and your sons live on the rest" (2 Kings 4:7, NKJV).

She had it all along. She was looking for Elisha to give her more, but she was carrying the ingredients for more in her hand. The moment she recognized her potential it empowered her to create more in her moment of pain, frustration, confusion and despair. In turn a new moment was born: one of prosperity, power, and restoration.

How often have you reached outside of yourself for resources you already possessed? You already carry what you desire to see. In other words, you are equipped with every resource you need to create and obtain *more* in this moment.

WALK IN

If you are going to create more, "the greater you" must seize the moment. You must enter the moment instead of waiting to be invited. So many people spend their lives waiting for permission to *live their lives*. We have been consistently taught to postpone our dreams and do what is "practical." We timidly stand outside the door of opportunities, hoping to be invited in, when all we need to do is walk in. In her book, *Lean In: Women, Work, and the Will to Lead*, Sheryl Sandberg says that as women, "we hold ourselves back in ways both big and small, by lacking self-confidence, by not raising our hands and by pulling back when we should be leaning in."[26]

I spent years standing on the sidelines of life, waiting for someone to invite me to do more with my life. I desperately wanted to be discovered. I yearned for someone important to open a door and give me permission to go to the next level I always knew existed in me. Then one day as I spouted my anger at God because it seemed nothing good ever happened to me, I sensed Him saying, "While you have been waiting on me to open a door, I have been waiting on you to walk in the door that's already been opened." Your dream represents an open door. You don't need permission to walk through a door God has opened. You don't need someone else to "greenlight" the life you have been called to. Don't let fear, insecurity, and doubt keep you stuck outside an open door. Give *yourself* permission to walk into your destiny.

HAVING THE AUDACITY

"What if I told you that after today you will never have to worry about failure?"

After I asked a client that question she smiled, sighed, and replied, "I could do anything!"

Imagine if rejection, denial, and failure no longer existed for you. What would your very next step be? Who would you become? What could you accomplish?

Any answer you give that doesn't align with what you are doing and where you are heading now, is a sign that fear is holding you back. Courage is not the absence of fear. It is the audacity to take ownership of your potential and live it out to its fullest. Audacity is the boldness to run to the edge of the cliff, throw caution to the wind, and jump. It is the refusal to take "no" for an answer because everything in you is shouting "Yes!"

Living audaciously means that you have adjusted your confidence level to match the size of the dream you are chasing. My daughter and her generation have a word they use for this kind of attitude: Swagger. Often when she talks about someone she admires, she will say, "I like him because he walks with swagger." "Swagger" is the confidence (some may say overconfidence) a person exudes when entering a room with an air of stardom and greatness. Their bank statement may read zero but their self-esteem says "a million dollars." Audacity is the courage to act like you're already there before you get there.

—∞—

Audacity is needed when you have to enter your moment at a moment's notice. A few years ago I experienced this during my church's annual "Power of God Conference." It was the first night and the invited guest was a nationally-known speaker. There was a buzz in the air as people arrived early to the venue, excited to hear him. An hour before the service, however, I received a call from the conference coordinator.

"Niki, I am so sorry but Bishop is making me call you." Pause. "The guest speaker for tonight is unable to come. His flight was cancelled due to a hurricane and Bishop wants you to take his place." Another pause. "And he needs you here in the next thirty minutes."

I died a thousand deaths in under a minute. I thought it was a cruel joke. I was a speaker, yes. I desired a larger audience, yes. But I didn't feel ready for something that big. *How will people react when I walk in instead of him? How can I possibly measure up? Isn't this conference for pastors and leaders of churches? How do I qualify to tell them anything?* For fifteen minutes I resisted the call to enter the moment. I just knew I was going to fail.

My husband found me in the bathroom, my eyes red and swollen from crying, panic written all over my face.

"Niki," he said, "if God didn't think you were ready for this moment, He would have never created it for you."

Those few words challenged my faith and courage. *Do I believe that this is my moment? Do I have the courage to walk in it even though I feel unqualified? Can I do it now?*

It's one thing to walk boldly into a new season when you have had time to prepare and shore up your weaknesses. But audacity is tested when at a moment's notice you enter the biggest time of your life with confidence, security, and faith that either you have everything you need to make it through this moment or that what you lack, God will provide. I mounted the stage that night with trembling knees and a courage I had never before experienced—courage that came from understanding that God had crafted that moment just for me and He wanted me to embrace it.

OWN THE MOMENT

There is a difference between a defining moment and a destiny moment. A defining moment shapes who I am. A destiny moment reveals where God is taking me. Looking back, I realize that the "Power of God Conference" experience was my defining moment. It was to transform my thinking into how I am to own the moment and not let the moment own me.

Some opportunities will literally change the direction of your life. These moments often come suddenly, without any forewarning, leaving you no time to process, plan, or even think clearly. If you are not ready, you will allow the enormity of the moment to overshadow you.

To own the moment you must move beyond the struggle you experienced in the process. At times we can allow the pain of the process to hinder us from entering the very thing we needed the process for. I wanted to stand on a larger platform, I spent years studying, praying and crying for an opportunity. But I had waited so long for the moment to come that I didn't recognize the moment when it arrived. I responded in fear rather than faith. Don't allow the pain of the journey to blind and hinder you from celebrating the promise when it comes. You may be *exactly* where God wants you. You may be walking in the manifestation of your dreams right now. If so, *own the moment.*

How you prepare for the moment will determine how you enter it, and how you own it. It takes consistency and faith. You have to believe that it's coming even during the dry seasons when it doesn't look like it. To prepare for the moment you must:

Prepare your mind and heart. Tell your heart and mind that something greater is coming. Tell yourself that not only is a great opportunity coming, but you have the capacity to walk in it. God will seldom release a blessing if we have not prepared the atmosphere for it. What you believe about yourself determines the atmosphere you create. When you believe that you are a carrier of greatness, you will create an atmosphere for greatness. God told His people, in Deuteronomy 28:2, "All these blessings shall come upon you and overtake you" (NKJV). I believe that when our hearts and minds are in a believing posture it is impossible for opportunities not to show up.

Perfect your passion. You have heard that "practice makes perfect." The truth of the statement depends a lot on your definition of "perfect." But practice does make you prepared. Practice your passion as often as you can. For several years I was not being invited to speak in formal settings. While I waited for those opportunities, however, I volunteered to teach in my church's Sunday school ministry. I volunteered in women's shelters and taught countless teen groups. I took a public speaking course. I read countless books on speaking. The more I practiced, the better I became.

Take advantage of seasons when there is little activity. Use those times to hone your craft. Volunteer your services and ask for feedback. Put yourself in positions where you can use your gift. Be intentional about preparing for the coming moment. When your moment comes, you won't have time to go back and practice.

Pray without ceasing. Prayer helps us to stay centered and connected to the plans and heartbeat of God. Prayer positions us in an intimate space with God where we have the opportunity to grow in faith and dependence on Him. When your faith grows, so does your capacity to handle unexpected opportunities. Prayer helps us confront hidden fears while also creating inner confirmation that we can do all things through Christ who strengthens us (Philippians 4:13).

Show Up. Your defining moment is not shaped by what opportunity presents itself—or when—but on *how* you, "the greater you" shows up in that moment. When the curtain goes up, will the world see you in the spotlight—or still hiding in the wings? How will you show up? You may have spent your entire life waiting in the wings for an opportunity to be more. Or maybe at one time you had more, but through circumstances feel like you lost it. God has been preparing you for a *new* moment. Don't remain stuck in the snapshot image of your past. Don't allow your doubts and fears to keep you trapped in your limitations. You are more. You can have more.

"The greater you" has been shaped in the matrix of God's will. It has an indomitable spirit. In the face of trouble, "the greater you" will deliberately show up with hope, expectancy, love, creativity, and gratitude. "The greater you" has the discipline to be present in this moment and every one that follows. "The greater you" is fully aware of who you are and stands tall in that knowledge. "The greater you" has the courage to be consistently authentic in every phase, stage, and season of your life, where there is continuity between who the world sees and who you really are.

This is your moment, right now. That one moment to do something your heart has been yearning for. You were born for this. Everything you have experienced; the trials, triumphs, mishaps and mistakes has prepared you for this moment to *receive* more. When you bring all of who you are into this moment you will finally see your dreams and desires come to life—because, in this moment, *you* will be creating them.

SKILL BUILDER

QUESTIONS FOR REFLECTION

1. What season are you in? Sowing, reaping, or harvesting?
2. What moments or opportunities is God calling you to step into in this season?
3. What steps can you take to prepare for the *next* moment?
4. How can you practice your passion?

CHAPTER 16

Make Your Move

———— ✆ ————

Do you want to know who you are? Don't ask.
Act! Action will delineate and define you

(Thomas Jefferson).

Y ou made it! You've read the book. You've walked the PATH.
You get it. So now what? Are you ready to create more for
your life? Do you know what greatness looks like?

Most successful people don't stumble into their success;
they schedule it. They put it on their calendar and most importantly, they have a plan.

What about faith? Can't we just believe for good things to
show up in our lives? Yes, but James 2:14 tells us, "Faith without
works is dead" (NKJV). Faith determines your actions. Your actions produce your outcome. Trying to create success without
a plan is like taking a road trip with no directions. You may get
there, but you may not.

Most people want more. They may even have a vague idea
of what more would look like. But it is much harder to follow a
path that hasn't been mapped.

Here are a couple steps you can take now to route your way
to a life of intentional greatness:

Develop SMART goals. The acronym SMART was popularized by management guru Peter Drucker. It is a common tool to clarify your focus and create momentum toward setting and achieving your goals. Your goals should be:

* **Specific** – What do you want to accomplish? Be clear about your target.
* **Measurable** – If you can't measure your progress, how will you know when you have accomplished your goal? So set measurable goals. Establish criteria for assessing your progress? For example, "I want to read more" is too general. But "I want to read at least three books this month" provides a helpful measurement.
* **Attainable** – Is your goal realistic? For example, wanting to lose forty pounds in two weeks is unrealistic. It only sets you up for failure. What is a more achievable target you are willing to work for?
* **Relevant** – How will achieving this goal affect your purpose? Make sure your goals are connected to your overall objective, the destination you are trying to reach.
* **Time Specific** – What's the deadline? Your goals should have a reasonable timeframe (such as "three books *this month*"). Setting a deadline reinforces the seriousness of what you want and motivates you to take action. When you don't set a deadline—or even multiple deadlines—there is no internal pressure to accomplish the goal, so it is easily put on the back burner. Look at where you are in this season of your life and make a reasonable estimate as to when your goal will be accomplished.

Take out a sheet of paper and start sketching out your SMART goals. Start with a simple, short-term goal you would like to achieve. For example:

NOT a SMART goal:
I want to increase my social media presence.

SMART goal:
In order to market my business product to more people, within the next 2 months, I will increase my presence on social media by posting 3 times a day and gaining 100 more likes on my fan page.

CREATE A BOARD OF DIRECTORS...FOR YOUR LIFE.

My friend Theresa Daniels Dozier wrote a book titled, *CEO of Your Life*. She helps women to re-structure their thinking by taking back control of their present and their future goals. But a CEO needs a board of directors to help guide the vision and direction of the organization.

Every woman needs a board of directors (BOD) in her life—a group of people who truly care about your success spiritually, personally, and professionally, and whose insight and opinions matter to you. More importantly, your BOD will help you stay true to your values, guard your priorities, and stay on the PATH when life threatens to derail you. Your BOD should have permission to be fearlessly truthful and give you periodic "reality checks" that may be uncomfortable but necessary.

Take out a piece of paper. Go ahead. I'll wait.

On that paper, jot the names of three to five people who have your love and respect, who have been honest with you in the past, whose values and perspectives you trust, and who have added something important to your life. Ideally, the people on this list should reflect a variety of backgrounds, experiences, and expertise. But they should have this in common: Wanting to see "the greater you" succeed and creating a life of intentional, deliberate greatness.

Once you have a working list, decide on (1) what you need from the board. For example do you need individual encouragement, guidance, and support from each board member? If so, you may invite them to rotate one-on-one meetings for that purpose. Or do you need to connect with them as a group on a monthly, weekly or quarterly basis? You may also commit to sending periodic updates on your progress via email, to which you would have them to respond with suggestions or support. The structure, of course, depends on what would be most helpful in this season of your life. (2) Also decide what area of your life you need your BOD: professionally, personally, or spiritually. Develop a SMART goal and use that as your platform for discussion.

Finally once you have decided what you will ask of the people on your list, decide how you will enlist them. Will you call each one individually? Will you email the whole group? Will you invite all of them to a dinner? Determine what you will ask of your board of directors and how you will make your "pitch." Then stay honest and faithful in communicating with them, helping them to help you stay true to your calling and destiny.

YOUR FUTURE IS WAITING

A life of greatness is not something in your distant future. You are standing in the PATH right now. The fact that you have gotten to this point of the book means you are already on the journey. Challenge your challenges and take your next step. When you move and take a risk you will be interrupting old patterns and starting new ones.

I believe that your next steps will be the most important you will ever take. They will start a domino effect that will create a series of events, encounters, decisions, open doors, and meetings that would never have been possible if you had remained still. You are not waiting for greatness to find you; "the greater you" is alive, present, and waiting to be revealed.

WORKS CITED

Introduction

1- "great." Oxford Dictionary.com. 2015. http://www.oxforddiction-airies.com/us/definition(Jan

2- Matthew 25:14-30.

3- See Matthew 25:15.

4- Mackay, Harvey. Made of Money. *Itsamoneything.com*. Daily Money Quotes.24 Jan.2015. Web. 24.2015.

Chapter 1

5- Paul Tillich. *The Courage to Be.*New Haven & London: Yale University Press,1952 Pg.46 Print.

Chapter 2

6- "Passion." *Meditation 24-7*. N.p., n.d. Web. 5 July 2015.

Chapter 3

7- Goldman Brian. "The Interrelated Roles Of Dispositional Authenticity, Self-Processes, And Global Role Functioning In Affecting Psychological Adjustment." (1995): 5. Web

8- Goleman D. (1997). Beyond IQ: developing the leadership competencies of emotional intelligence. Paper presented at the 2nd international competency conference, London, October.

9- Jakes, T D., *Instinct: The Power to Unleash Your Inborn Drive.* New York: Faith Words, 2014. Pg14. Print.

10- Robbins, Mike., *Be Yourself, Everyone Else is Already Taken.* San Franciso, CA: Josey Bass, 2009.

11- "Zusya Archives - Rabbi David Kominsky" *Home - Rabbi David Kominsky.* N.p., 22 Aug. 2012. Web. 5 July 2015.

Chapter 4

12- Thurman, Chris. *The Lies We Believe.* Nashville: T. Nelson, 1989. Pg. 5. Print.

Chapter 5

13- "Transparent | Definition of Transparent by Merriam-Webster." *Dictionary and Thesaurus | Merriam-Webster.* N.p., n.d. Web. 5 July 2015.

Chapter 7

14- Maxwell, John C. *The 21 Irrefutable Laws of Leadership.* Nashville: Thomas Nelson, 2007. Pg. 90 Print.

15- Maxwell, John C.and Jim Dornan. *Becoming a Person of Influence: How to Positively Impact the Lives of Others.* Nashville: T. Nelson Publishers, 1997. Back cover copy. Print.

Chapter 9

16- McKeown, Greg. *Essentialism: The Disciplined Pursuit of Less.* Crown Business, 2014. Pg.4. Kindle.

17- IBID pg.16

18- Keller, Gary. *The One Thing.* London: Hachette Book Group, 2013. Pg 18. Print.

Chapter 10

19- Williamson, Marianne. "Marianne Williamson." *Wikiquote.* N.p., n.d. Web.

Chapter 12

20- McLeod, Shawn R. *"The Cheat Sheet for Creating Vision Boards That Lead to Discovering Your Purpose."* In *Voices of the 21st Century,* by Theresa Dozier-Daniel, 249-265. Bridgeport: Hope of Vision Publishing, 2013. Pg 4. Print

21- Confucius. "Quote by Confucius: "True Wisdom is Knowing What You Don't Know"." *Goodreads.* N.p., n.d. Web.

22- Buckingham, Marcus, and Donald O. Clifton. *Now, Discover Your Strengths.* New York: Free Press, 2001. Pg 26. Print.

23- Lee, Charles. *Good Idea. Now What? How to Move Ideas to Execution.* Hoboken: Wiley, 2012. Pg. 23. Print.

Chapter 13

24- Chand, Samuel R, and Cecil B. Murphey. *Who Moved Your Ladder? Your Next Bold Move.* Niles: Mall Publishing, 2006. Pg.2 Kindle

Chapter 15

25- Jodi Kantor. *A Titan's How-To on Breaking the Glass Ceiling;* 21 FEB. 2013. Web.21.2013

Made in the USA
Middletown, DE
22 April 2019